# AQA HISTORY

# GCSE 9–1

# Germany, 1890–1945: Democracy and Dictatorship

by Rob Bircher

# ■SCHOLASTIC

**Author** Rob Bircher

**Reviewer** Paul Martin

**Editorial team** Rachel Morgan, Aidan Gill, Vicki Yates, Deborah Hey, Caroline Low

**Typesetting** Daniel Prescott, Couper Street Type Co.

**Cover design** Dipa Mistry

**App development** Hannah Barnett, Phil Crothers and RAIOSOFT International Pvt Ltd

**Photographs**

Photographs page 10: Paul von Hindenburg, Everett Historical/Shutterstock; pages 10 and 14: Kaiser Wilhelm II, Everett Historical/Shutterstock; pages 10 and 23: Gustav Stresemann, German Federal Archives/Wikimedia Commons; pages 10 and 30: Franz von Papen, German Federal Archives/ Wikimedia Commons; page 11: Adolf Hitler, Ernst Röhm, German Federal Archives/Wikimedia Commons; pages 11 and 40: Joseph Goebbels, German Federal Archives/Wikimedia Commons; pages 11 and 46: Heinrich Himmler, German Federal Archives/Wikimedia Commons; page 14: SMS Kaiser, German Federal Archives/Wikimedia Commons; page 15: Kaiser Wilhelm cartoon, National WWI Museum and Memorial, USA; page 17: lamb, Pozdeyev Vitaly/Shutterstock; page 18: poster, Chronicle/Alamy Stock Photo; page 19: French soldiers, Shutterstock; page 20: bank notes as building blocks, Pictorial Press Ltd/Alamy; page 24: couple dancing, Everett Collection/Shutterstock; page 25: Herman Müller, German Federal Archives/Wikimedia Commons; Heinrich Brüning, German Federal Archives/Wikimedia Commons; German worker, Everett Historical/Shutterstock; page 26: Adolf Hitler, Ivor Golovniov/Alamy; page 35: The SA, World History Archive/Alamy; page 36: road construction, Everett Historical/Shutterstock; page 40: Nazi propaganda poster, Glasshouse Images/Alamy; page 41: Hitler Youth, German Federal Archives/Wikimedia Commons; page 74: girl sitting exam, Monkey Business Images/Shutterstock

**Illustration** QBS Learning

Designed using Adobe InDesign

Published in the UK by Scholastic Education, 2020
Book End, Range Road, Witney, Oxfordshire, OX29 0YD
A division of Scholastic Limited
London – New York – Toronto – Sydney – Auckland
Mexico City – New Delhi – Hong Kong
SCHOLASTIC and associated logos are trademarks and/or registered trademarks of Scholastic Inc.
www.scholastic.co.uk
© 2020 Scholastic Limited
1 2 3 4 5 6 7 8 9   0 1 2 3 4 5 6 7 8 9

**British Library Cataloguing-in-Publication Data**
A catalogue record for this book is available from the British Library.

**ISBN 978-1407-18337-4**

Printed and bound by Bell and Bain Ltd, Glasgow
Papers used by Scholastic Limited are made from wood grown in sustainable forests.

**Acknowledgements**
The publishers gratefully acknowledge permission to reproduce the following copyright material: **Plunkett Lake Press** for 'A Dossier on my Former Self' from *Account Rendered* by Melita Maschmann, (Plunkett Lake Press, 2013)

Every effort has been made to trace copyright holders for the works reproduced in this book, and the publishers apologise for any inadvertent omissions.

**Note from the publisher:**
Please use this product in conjunction with the official specification and sample assessment materials. Ask your teacher if you are unsure where to find them.

Many thanks to Maisie and Kitty for testing out the questions in the *How to answer the AQA exam questions* section.

# Contents

**Check your answers on
the free revision app or at
www.scholastic.co.uk/gcse**

# Features of this guide

The best way to retain information is to take an active approach to revision.

Throughout this book, you will find lots of features that will make your revision an active, successful process.

## SNAPIT!

Use the Snap it! feature in the revision app to take pictures of key concepts and information. Great for revision on the go!

Regular exercise helps stimulate the brain and will help you relax.

## DOIT!

Activities to embed your knowledge and understanding and prepare you for the exams.

Find methods of relaxation that work for you throughout the revision period.

## NAILIT!

Succinct and vital tips on how to do well in your exam.

Words shown in **purple bold** can be found in the glossary on page 76.

## STRETCHIT!

Provides content that stretches you further.

## CHECKIT!

Check your knowledge at the end of a subtopic.

Revise in pairs or small groups and deliver presentations on topics to each other.

## PRACTICE PAPERS

Full mock-exam papers to practise before you sit the real thing!

FOR HIGH-MARK QUESTIONS, SPEND TIME **PLANNING** YOUR ANSWER!

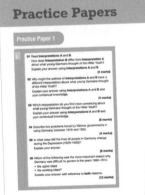

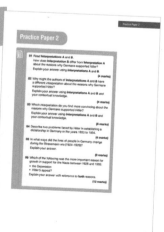

## FREE REVISION APP

- The **free revision app** can be downloaded to your mobile phone (iOS and Android), making **on the go revision** easy.

- Use the revision calendar to help map out your revision in the lead-up to the exam.

- Complete multiple-choice questions and create your own **SNAPIT!** revision cards.

**www.scholastic.co.uk/gcse**

**Online answers and additional resources**
All of the tasks in this book are designed to get you thinking and to consolidate your understanding through thought and application. Therefore, it is important to write your own answers before checking. Some questions include answer lines where you need to fill in your answer in the book. Other questions require you to use a separate piece of paper so that you can draft your response and work out the best way of answering.

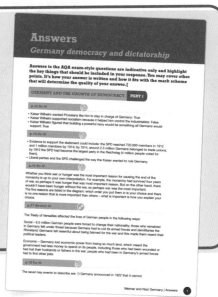

Get plenty of sleep, especially the night before an exam.

## LOOK AFTER YOURSELF

Help your brain by looking after your whole body!

Once you have worked through a section, you can check your answers to Do it!, Stretch it!, Check it! and the exam practice papers on the app or at **www.scholastic.co.uk/gcse**.

# Topic focus:
## Modern depth study

The Germany 1890–1945 topic is a period study. This means you will have focused on one country, Germany, for a period of around 50 years – a period in which the country experienced massive changes. You will have studied the impacts these major developments had on people, looking at different perspectives for how these changes were shaped as well as their impacts.

## Causation and consequences

Your exam will have a question focused on **consequences**: the results of something happening. Question 5 asks you to explain in what way the lives of people were affected by something – what the consequences for people were.

Your exam will also have a question focused on **causation**: reasons why something happened. Question 6 asks you to explain why one of two reasons was more important than the other in causing something.

Causes and consequences can be complex. For example, the economic consequences of a government policy can be positive, but some social consequences can be negative, for instance for some groups in society. Causes and consequences can be political, social, cultural and economic. They can also relate to the role of ideas and be influenced by the contributions of key individuals and groups of people.

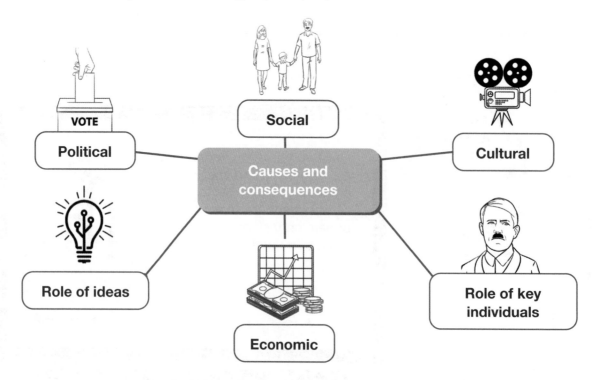

# Interpretations

You will also study **interpretations**. These are short pieces of text, around 50 to 100 words long, (they are always written and never pictures) which look at an aspect of your course from different points of view. There are also always some details about who wrote them.

You will need to identify a difference between two interpretations, suggest a reason why they might be different and then consider which of the two interpretations you think is the most convincing.

| **Interpretation 1:** | **Interpretation 2:** |
|---|---|
| The reason Hitler came to power in 1933 was because of the political deals of Papen and Schleicher with President Hindenburg. Without them, he would have never gained power. | The reason Hitler came to power in 1933 was because of the Great Depression and subsequent unemployment. This economic crisis led to huge support for the Nazis that could not be ignored. |

**What is the difference between the interpretations?**

The interpretations each give a different key reason as to how Hitler came to power.

**Why might they be different?**

Reasons could include:

- they were written by people with different political views
- one might be written by someone closely connected with events, the other not
- they are different sorts of documents, for example one is a private diary and the other a speech
- the interpretations were written for different reasons.

**Which interpretation is more convincing?**

You will need to draw on your own knowledge to decide which interpretation you find the most convincing. If one interpretation agrees with most of what you already know about the topic, then that is the one that will be the most convincing for you.

# Timeline

## Germany and the growth of democracy

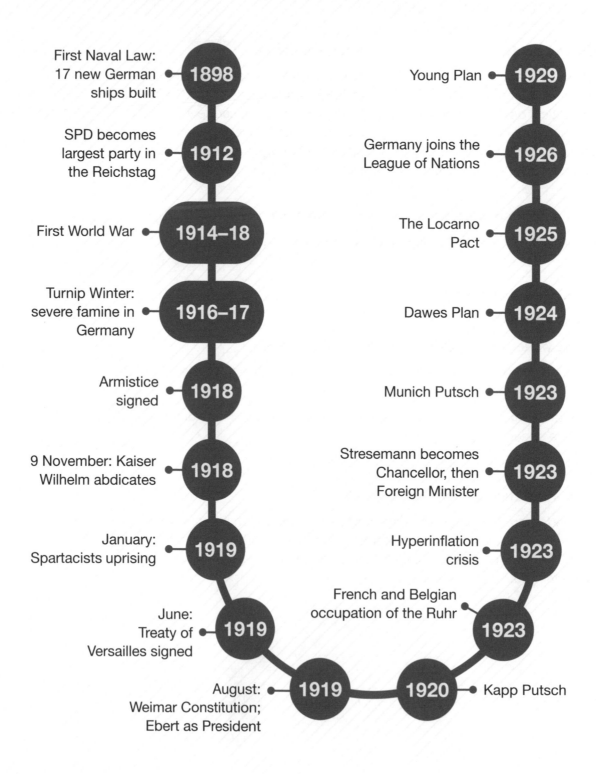

First Naval Law: 17 new German ships built — **1898**

SPD becomes largest party in the Reichstag — **1912**

First World War — **1914–18**

Turnip Winter: severe famine in Germany — **1916–17**

Armistice signed — **1918**

9 November: Kaiser Wilhelm abdicates — **1918**

January: Spartacists uprising — **1919**

June: Treaty of Versailles signed — **1919**

August: Weimar Constitution; Ebert as President — **1919**

**1920** — Kapp Putsch

**1923** — French and Belgian occupation of the Ruhr

Hyperinflation crisis — **1923**

Stresemann becomes Chancellor, then Foreign Minister — **1923**

Munich Putsch — **1923**

Dawes Plan — **1924**

The Locarno Pact — **1925**

Germany joins the League of Nations — **1926**

Young Plan — **1929**

## Germany and the Depression

**1929** — Wall Street Crash: Depression begins

**1930** — Nazis achieve 18% of vote in national elections

**1932** — Unemployment reaches 6 million

**1932** — NSDAP becomes largest party in the Reichstag with 37% of vote

**1933** — Hitler appointed as Chancellor

**1933** — Reichstag Fire

**1933** — Enabling Act

**1934** — Night of the Long Knives

**1934** — Death of Hindenburg. Hitler becomes Führer

**1939** — Germany invades Poland; Second World War begins

## The experiences of Germans under the Nazis

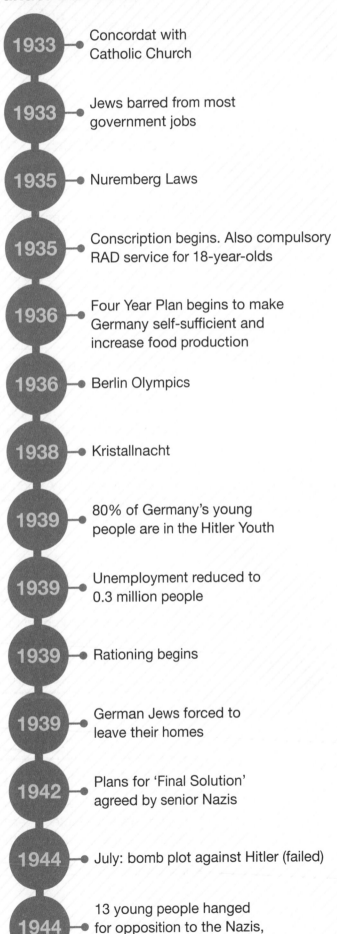

1933 — Concordat with Catholic Church

1933 — Jews barred from most government jobs

1935 — Nuremberg Laws

1935 — Conscription begins. Also compulsory RAD service for 18-year-olds

1936 — Four Year Plan begins to make Germany self-sufficient and increase food production

1936 — Berlin Olympics

1938 — Kristallnacht

1939 — 80% of Germany's young people are in the Hitler Youth

1939 — Unemployment reduced to 0.3 million people

1939 — Rationing begins

1939 — German Jews forced to leave their homes

1942 — Plans for 'Final Solution' agreed by senior Nazis

1944 — July: bomb plot against Hitler (failed)

1944 — 13 young people hanged for opposition to the Nazis, including Edelweiss Pirates

# Key figures

## Kaiser Wilhelm II (1859–1941)

Kaiser Wilhelm II became the leader of Germany in 1888, when he was 29 years old. He was forced to abdicate in 1918.

Wilhelm loved the military and was convinced that Germany's army could defeat any other country. He believed the German aristocracy should govern Germany and hated the idea of sharing any power with ordinary people.

## Gustav Stresemann (1878–1929)

Stresemann was Chancellor for around three months in 1923, during which time he acted to end Germany's hyperinflation crisis. He was then foreign minister from 1923 to 1929. In this time he helped to improve relations between Germany and the Allied powers.

## Fritz von Papen (1879–1969)

Papen is best known for the political deal that let Hitler become Chancellor. Papen underestimated Hitler, thinking he could control him. Instead, Hitler quickly expanded his powers.

## Paul von Hindenburg (1847–1934)

Hindenburg was a war hero of the First World War. In 1925, he was elected President of the Weimar Republic, after the death of the first President, Friedrich Ebert.

## Adolf Hitler (1889–1945)

Adolf Hitler fought in the First World War, was wounded in the Battle of the Somme and received a medal for bravery. Hitler's first attempt to gain power in Germany failed when he was imprisoned for treason (the Munich Putsch). While in prison he wrote *Mein Kampf* ('My Struggle'), which spread his racist beliefs and hatred of Jews. Hitler's Nazi Party grew in popularity after Germany was plunged into an economic and social crisis in the Depression, and in 1933 Hitler achieved his ambition of becoming German Chancellor, which he then used to gain complete power as Germany's Führer. As dictator, Hitler set about rebuilding the German economy, removing any opposition to Nazi control, establishing a Nazi culture, rebuilding Germany's military strength, and using threats and intimidation to take territory from other countries. Eventually his aggressive actions brought about the Second World War. After starting off the war with amazing successes, Hitler's decision to attack the USSR eventually led to Germany's complete defeat. Hitler committed suicide in a bunker in Berlin in April 1945.

## Joseph Goebbels (1897–1945)

Hitler made Goebbels the director of Nazi Party propaganda in 1927, and Goebbels kept this role throughout the Nazis' control of Germany.

## Heinrich Himmler (1900–1945)

When Himmler was put in charge of Hitler's bodyguard, the SS, he expanded it into a force of 50,000 men. Himmler also became chief of the Gestapo, the Nazis' secret police force. During the Second World War, he organised the system that murdered 6 million Jews.

## Ernst Röhm (1887–1934)

Rohm co-founded the SA ('stormtroopers') and was its leader from 1931 until the Night of the Long Knives in 1934, when he was murdered on Hitler's orders.

# Part One:
## Germany and the growth of democracy

## How was Germany governed under Kaiser Wilhelm?

Wilhelm II was the **Kaiser** of Germany. He did not allow the **Reichstag** to interfere with his decisions on how Germany should be governed.

- The Kaiser chose who was Chancellor and could also decide to sack the Chancellor and shut down the Reichstag if he didn't like their decisions.

- The Chancellor controlled the government – like the Prime Minister in Britain. The Chancellor did need to get the Reichstag to agree new laws but he could ignore the Reichstag's views if he wanted to. The Chancellor was always a **Prussian**.

- Reichstag representatives were elected: all German men over the age of 25 had a vote. However, the Reichstag's powers were weak. Its main role was to discuss new laws, put forward by the Kaiser and his government, not to make new laws itself.

### Why was Germany difficult to rule?

The Kaiser was a Prussian and wanted to keep Germany under the control of the Prussian elite, but Germany was changing. **Industrialisation** created new social and political pressures, as described in the table at the top of page 13.

### Who were the Prussians?

Rich Prussian landowners had controlled Germany's government and military since Germany became a country in 1871. The German royal family were Prussians.

The Prussian elite had always been able to control Germany's peasants, because they owned their land. But now peasants were leaving the land to work in factories in towns and cities. As a result of industrialisation, Prussians felt they were losing power.

**NAILIT!**

This section of the course is focused on why Germany was difficult to rule before the First World War. Make sure you are clear on the different factors that contributed to this difficulty – industrialisation, socialism, parliamentary democracy, the Prussian elite and militarism.

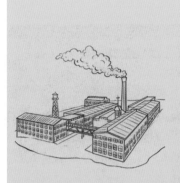

Industrialisation had made Germany wealthy in the 1890s. Not only was Germany important in industries like steel-making, it was also a world leader in new industries like chemicals and electronics.

Germany's government and military were controlled by Prussian landowners. They did not want to give up their control or share it with anyone else. But industrialisation was weakening their position.

Industrialisation created a new class of wealthy factory owners. They wanted the government to help them make more money. They also wanted a share of political power.

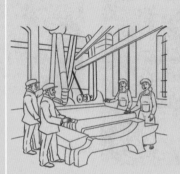

Industrialisation meant the number of industrial workers doubled between the 1880s and 1907. These were people who had been peasant farmers. Now they were in towns and cities, living and working in bad conditions. These people wanted the government to help them improve wages and conditions.

### Kaiser Wilhelm: Factfile

Kaiser Wilhelm was a Prussian and he wanted to keep Prussians in charge of Germany. He even wanted to take away voting rights from working people to stop the growth of a **socialist** political party, the **SPD**, that was popular with workers. But his advisers convinced him that doing this risked a revolution.

Instead, the Kaiser's government brought in **social reforms**, for example in 1891 the Social Law banned Sunday working and the employment of children under 13, in 1901 industrial arbitration courts were introduced to settle disputes between workers and employers, and in 1903 benefits for workers who could not work because of illness were introduced. The idea was that these reforms would keep the German workers happy, which meant that the Prussians could stay in control.

The Kaiser also tried to bring his country together through **nationalism** – for example, by building a powerful German navy and developing a German empire. Wilhelm figured that Germans from all classes would put aside their differences and work together to make Germany a great world power.

**DOIT!**

Read the following information about how Kaiser Wilhelm tried to govern Germany and then circle True or False:

- Kaiser Wilhelm wanted Prussians like him to stay in charge of Germany. [True/False]

- Kaiser Wilhelm supported socialism because it helped him control the industrialists. [True/False]

- Kaiser Wilhelm figured that building a powerful navy would be something all Germans would support. [True/False]

## Challenges for Kaiser Wilhelm

### The growth of socialism

The government's attempts to use social reforms (see previous page) to stop the growth of socialism didn't work. Socialism kept growing.

- The SPD reached 720,000 members in 1912 and 1 million members by 1914.

- By 1914, around 2.5 million Germans belonged to trade unions. Many of them went on strike to demand higher wages and better working conditions.

- By 1912 the SPD became the largest party in the Reichstag: 4 million people voted for them.

Socialism made the workers powerful and threatened the industrialists and the Prussian elite.

### The difficulties of parliamentary government

Different political parties had different aims.

- The Conservatives supported the Kaiser and the Prussian elite.

- Liberal parties wanted power to be taken away from the elite and used to help industrialists.

- The SPD wanted workers to be in charge of Germany.

Divisions in the Reichstag showed that Germany was divided, making it more difficult to rule.

## The Navy Laws

**1.** In 1897 Germany's navy was the seventh largest in the world. By 1914 it was the second largest (Britain's navy was the largest).

**2.** This rapid growth was because Kaiser Wilhelm was obsessed with Germany becoming a world power, which meant having a navy that could challenge Britain's navy.

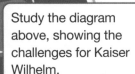

Study the diagram above, showing the challenges for Kaiser Wilhelm.

- 'Socialism was growing under Kaiser Wilhelm's rule'. Find evidence to support this statement.

- Which political parties challenged the way Kaiser Wilhelm wanted to rule Germany?

**5.** The expansion of the navy worried Britain, which began expanding its navy, too. So the Navy Laws increased international tensions.

**4.** Different political parties in the Reichstag supported the Navy Laws. This helped with governing Germany.

**3.** The Navy Laws gave the government money to build more ships. The first Navy Law in 1898 was for money to build 17 battleships in seven years. The Kaiser wanted more, and new laws were passed in 1900 (36 ships), 1906, 1908 and 1912.

# The impact of the First World War

In November 1918 German politicians and military leaders signed the **armistice** that ended the First World War. The peace deal was very bad for Germany, but the country was isolated (its allies had surrendered) and German people were starving. On 9 November, Kaiser Wilhelm **abdicated**.

## Why was Kaiser Wilhelm forced to abdicate?

**1** War weariness: two million Germans had been killed in fighting and four million were wounded. So much had been sacrificed.

**2** 750,000 Germans died in 1918 because they could not get enough to eat. There were not enough men and horses to work the farms (they were all in the army), a very cold autumn and winter in 1916–17 destroyed crops, and the British navy stopped ships carrying food supplies reaching German ports. People were angry that the government did nothing to help.

**5** Economic crisis: Wilhelm's government had no money: the government owed 150 billion marks in debts. Wilhelm had refused to increase taxes to pay for the war because he was so sure Germany would win it.

### Reasons for the Kaiser's abdication

**4** Kaiser Wilhelm's government had lost control of the country: by 6 November, workers' and soldiers' councils had taken control of many German towns away from the Kaiser's officials. This was known as the November Revolution.

**3** Kaiser Wilhelm lost the support of the German armed forces: for example, there was a navy mutiny in Kiel in October 1918. Soldiers and sailors could see the war was lost and did not want to continue fighting.

Cartoon from 1916 showing Kaiser Wilhelm II standing between the spectral figures of War and Hunger.

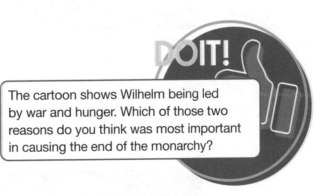

DOIT!

The cartoon shows Wilhelm being led by war and hunger. Which of those two reasons do you think was most important in causing the end of the monarchy?

## Post-war problems: the Treaty of Versailles

The Treaty of Versailles was the peace treaty that ended the First World War. The Treaty was signed on 28 June 1919. Even before it was signed, it caused major problems for the new, post-war government of Germany.

> The German people expected a fair peace treaty for all sides. After all, Germany had launched a major offensive in spring 1918 that nearly won the war. The US President had also stressed the need for a fair peace treaty.

> Discussions on the peace treaty began in January 1919, but Germany was not allowed to take part. The Treaty's terms would be decided by Germany's enemies.

> In May 1919, the Germans were shocked by a draft version of the Treaty. The leader of the new Weimar government resigned rather than agree to its harsh terms. The new leader tried to get some of the worst bits taken out of the Treaty.

> The Allies told the German government that their armies would invade Germany if its government did not sign the Treaty just as it was. The German government representatives reluctantly signed the Treaty. Many Germans called the representatives the 'November criminals' because they thought that in signing the Treaty they had betrayed Germany.

### Why was the Treaty of Versailles such a problem?

The Treaty of Versailles contained 440 different 'articles' or terms covering many different aspects of the peace settlement. The key problems for Germany in the Treaty are outlined on the following page.

## STRETCHIT!

How did the Treaty of Versailles affect the lives of German people? (Hint: think social and economic – plus political).

Germany lost 13% of its territory. For example, Germany had to return Alsace-Lorraine to France.

**Economic impacts**: the lost lands had produced around 50% of all Germany's iron ore, 15% of its coal and 15% of its farm production.

**Social impacts**: 12% of Germany's population (6.5 million people) lived in these lost land.

- Germany had to cut its army to 100,000 soldiers.
- Its navy could only have six battleships and no submarines.
- It was not allowed military aircraft.
- **Conscription** was not allowed.
- The Rhineland area on France's border had to be demilitarised.

- Germany had to accept that it was to blame for the war (the War Guilt clause, Article 231).
- Accepting blame meant that Germany had to take responsibility for all the damage caused to its enemies – and pay them reparations.

**Land**

**Blame**

**Treaty of Versailles: impacts on Germany**

**Army**

**Money**

**Economic impacts**: Germany had to pay reparations.

**Social impacts**: German people did not believe they had started the war. This made the Treaty seem unfair and the majority of Germans resented it.

**Economic impacts**: German war industries declined.

**Social impacts**: German people did not feel safe. Germans felt their country was no longer a respected 'great power'. People who lost their jobs couldn't go into the army.

Germany had to pay **reparations** to compensate for war damage. This was set at £6600 million.

**Economic impacts**: Germany was already in debt. Not all reparations were in money: e.g. until 1935 all coal from Germany's Saar region had to go to France. This meant less coal for German industry.

**Social impacts**: Money spent on reparations could not be used to help the German people, e.g. pensions for soldiers wounded in the war.

**DO IT!**

Take a picture of this lamb. Add annotations to it for the impacts of the Treaty of Versailles: **L**and, **A**rmy, **M**oney and **B**lame.

Use the mnemonic to help you remember treaty's impacts.

# Post-war problems: the occupation of the Ruhr

## Why was the Ruhr occupied in 1923?

This German poster from 1923 has the worker saying to the French troops, 'No, you cannot force me'.

In 1922, the German government announced that its economic problems meant it could not afford to pay reparations for the next three years.

France and Belgium did not believe the German government was telling the truth. They decided to use force to get their reparations from Germany.

In January 1923, 60,000 French and Belgian troops occupied the Ruhr region of Germany. The Ruhr was an important industrial region.

The troops took control of factories, steelworks, railways and coalmines. The aim was to take the steel, coal and factory goods that the region produced as reparations.

The German government responded by encouraging workers in the Ruhr to go on strike. That way the French and Belgians would not be able to take its payments by force.

The German government continued to pay workers in the Ruhr their wages, so they would not suffer.

Although the French brought in their own workers, production in the Ruhr slumped. Troops were increased to over 100,000 because of German **sabotage** operations. The German people supported the government's actions, bringing the nation closer together.

French troops seize iron pipe in the Ruhr as part of the payment of reparations.

## Consequences for Germany

The German government's strategy of resisting the occupation caused major problems for the German economy – which was already under strain because of war debts. In fact, the costs to the economy were two times bigger than the cost of paying reparations that year.

Because the Ruhr's factories weren't making anything, there were shortages of different kinds of products. This meant prices for these products went up.

Businesses in the Ruhr that had shut down were not paying taxes to the government, and nor were striking workers. This meant money was not coming in to the government.

**Consequences of the occupation**

Because the Ruhr wasn't producing coal, Germany had to import coal from other countries. This was very expensive for the government.

Paying wages to the striking workers took a lot of money, which the government couldn't afford.

Close this book and go and tell someone the story of the occupation of the Ruhr. Remember, there are seven key events to describe.

**DO IT!**

What would each of these German people say about their experiences of hyperinflation?

- A businessman who wanted to expand his business
- A pensioner who lived off a state pension and their savings
- A housewife, responsible for feeding her family each day

## Hyperinflation!

### Why did hyperinflation happen?

- The German government was running out of money. However, it did not want to raise taxes as it would cause social and political problems.
- Instead, the government printed more money. It sold this money to buy foreign money, but that made the German currency worth less.
- Prices in German shops increased faster and faster as the currency became worth less and less. This is called hyperinflation.

### Consequences of hyperinflation

Prices rose so quickly that some workers had to be paid twice a day. At one point in October 1923, it cost 4 billion German marks to buy a dozen eggs – which had only cost half a mark each in 1918!

✗ Farmers did not sell their crops – what was the point when the money was worthless? This made it hard for people in the cities to find food to buy.

✗ People stopped using their worthless money and instead spent all day trying to find someone else who would swap what they had for food.

✗ People with savings did badly. Their savings lost all their value. What had been enough money to retire on in 1919 would not even buy a box of matches in 1923!

✗ People who lived off pensions and benefits suffered because their pensions and benefits did not increase.

✓ People with debts benefited from hyperinflation because it was very easy to pay back debts. (Reparations were different: they had to be paid in foreign currency.)

✓ Businesses could expand by taking out loans and then paying them back once the currency had lost even more value.

✓ Farmers were not hit so badly because they could grow food to eat – they didn't need money as much as workers.

**STRETCH IT!**

The best answers recognise that one factor often relates to other factors. Explain how hyperinflation was connected to the occupation of the Ruhr and the Treaty of Versailles.

### Who was to blame for hyperinflation?

Most Germans blamed their government for hyperinflation. The crisis led to more political unrest against the government – for example, the Munich **Putsch** (see page 21).

# The Weimar democracy

## Political change and unrest, 1919–1923

### The Spartacists (1919)

- When the new Weimar Republic began in 1918, the government was led by the socialist SPD. However, not all socialists agreed with each other. A group called the Spartacists wanted Germany to become **communist**. They formed a new party, the German Communist Party – KPD.

- In January 1919 the Spartacists tried to take over the government in Berlin. They wanted to make Germany a communist state.

- The leader of the Weimar government, President Ebert, did a deal with the army and also with the **Freikorps**, to put down the Spartacist rebellion. The Spartacists were easily defeated.

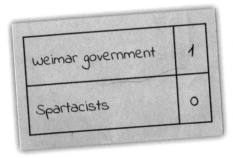

| | |
|---|---|
| weimar government | 1 |
| Spartacists | 0 |

### The Kapp Putsch (1920)

- In 1920 the Weimar government announced that the Freikorps would be banned and the size of the army reduced.

- The leader of the Berlin Freikorps, Walter von Lüttwitz, refused to obey. He got together with a right-wing politician, Wolfgang Kapp, and took control in Berlin.

- The Weimar government asked the army to take back control in Berlin, but the army refused.

- Ebert called on the workers of Berlin to go on strike against the putsch, which they did. The strikes meant Kapp's new government could get nothing done. The putsch collapsed after only 4 days.

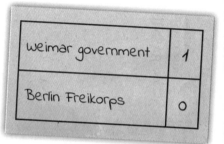

| | |
|---|---|
| weimar government | 1 |
| Berlin Freikorps | 0 |

### The Munich Putsch (November, 1923)

- The Munich Putsch was led by Adolf Hitler. He hated the way the Weimar government went along with the Treaty of Versailles. Hitler thought hyperinflation had convinced everyone in Germany that the Weimar government was useless.

- Hitler's plan was to take control in Bavaria first, because Bavaria's leaders did not think much of the Weimar government. Next would be Berlin.

- On 8 November 1923, Hitler led 600 **Nazis** into a huge beer hall in Munich, Bavaria, where Bavaria's three leaders were at a meeting. The three leaders were held at gunpoint until they agreed to support Hitler's putsch. Then they were set free.

- Two of the leaders then organised troops and police to put down the putsch. The Nazi Party was banned. Hitler was put on trial for treason and sentenced to 5 years in prison (but he actually only served 9 months).

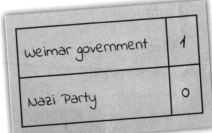

| | |
|---|---|
| weimar government | 1 |
| Nazi Party | 0 |

**DOIT!**

1 Describe:

  **a** one economic threat to the Weimar Republic

  **b** one political threat to the Weimar Republic.

2 'The fact that the Weimar government faced so many threats shows how weak it was.' Give one piece of evidence to support this statement, and one against it

## Weimar's 'Golden Years', 1924–1929

In 1923, Gustav Stresemann became Chancellor of Germany, then Foreign Minister in 1924. His aims were to reduce all the economic, social and political problems caused by the Treaty of Versailles.

### A new currency

Stresemann's government ended hyperinflation by introducing a new temporary currency: the Rentenmark, in November 1923. In 1924 it was converted into the Reichsmark.

- The amount of Rentenmarks was strictly limited. This stopped the government fuelling hyperinflation by printing more money.

- The Rentenmark was also backed up. If it failed, investors would get shares of land. This meant people trusted it as a currency. People started saving in banks again.

Although the new currency succeeded in ending hyperinflation, introducing it was painful. The Reichstag forced Stresemann to resign as Chancellor.

### The Dawes Plan

In 1923, Stresemann called off German resistance in the Ruhr and agreed to start making reparation payments again. This was popular with other countries and led to the USA coming up with the Dawes Plan (1924) to help Germany recover.

| What did the Dawes Plan do? | What were the results of the Dawes Plan? |
|---|---|
| Reparation payments were reduced to amounts that Germany would be able to pay: starting at $50 million per year for the first five years. | France was pleased that reparation payments would continue. The occupation of the Ruhr ended in 1925. |
| The USA loaned Germany $200 million. | German businesses could expand again (including those in the Ruhr), creating jobs and wealth. As German industries expanded, more and more US investment flowed into the country: nearly $3000 million by 1930. Almost all Germans benefited. |

The Dawes Plan was very successful in the short term. The German economy recovered quickly and Germans were better off. However, the German economy became dependent on US loans, which had bad long-term consequences.

## The Young Plan (1930)

Although the Dawes Plan reduced yearly reparation payments, the German government continued to complain that it could not afford reparations. In 1929, Stresemann signed the Young Plan, which reduced the total amount from £6600 million to £1850 million, and gave Germany another 59 years to pay.

**DO IT!**

1 Write a 'to do' list for Stresemann in 1923. What did he want to achieve for Germany?

2 For each point on your list, decide how successful he was in achieving his aims.

## International agreements

For Stresemann, Germany's recovery depended on minimising the impacts of the Treaty of Versailles. The first step for this was to get better relations between Germany and Britain and France.

- **The Locarno Pact (1925)**: Germany agreed to respect its borders with Belgium and France. This meant France could feel safer about its future relations with Germany. *This was important because* it meant cooperation between Germany and France improved, e.g. the end of occupation of the Ruhr.

- **Joining the League of Nations (1926)**: Germany had been kept out of the League of Nations when it formed in 1920. In 1926, Germany was invited to join. *This was important because* it helped Stresemann negotiate the Young Plan (1929), which further reduced reparation payments.

**STRETCH IT!**

Write an obituary for Stresemann in 1929 with the headline 'Gustav Stresemann (1878–1929): Was he the saviour of the Weimar Republic?'

## Weimar Culture

- Women had more freedom to express themselves during the Weimar era, e.g. they could choose to have short haircuts, shorter skirts and wear more makeup.

- Women went out on their own and drank alcohol and smoked in public. These changes were linked to the Weimar government's socialist policies, which gave women more status, more leisure time and more money.

- Women over 20 got the vote in 1919 and had equal rights to men in education and equal pay in some jobs. However, some Germans, for example the Nazis, hated these changes.

Cinema was very popular, with German film directors developing new special effects. A German actress, Marlene Dietrich, became world famous. Listening to the radio was popular: a quarter of all Germans owned a radio by 1932.

Cabaret clubs showcased jazz music, new dance crazes and edgy humour that mocked every aspect of German society. This permissive culture shocked more traditional Germans. Racists hated the link between black American culture and these new fashions because of their racist ideology.

# CHECKIT! ✔

1  Describe two ways in which Kaiser Wilhelm controlled the German government.

2  Describe three negative impacts of the Treaty of Versailles on Germany.

3  Explain two reasons for the end of the monarchy in Germany.

4  Identify four ways in which hyperinflation affected people's lives in Germany in 1923.

5  Describe three actions taken by Stresemann that helped Germany's recovery, 1924–29.

6  Explain one weakness in Germany's recovery.

# Part Two:
## Germany and the Depression

## The impact of the Depression

The Wall Street Crash in the USA led to a worldwide **depression**. Countries spent less, which meant German businesses lost export orders. Without US loans or exports, German businesses were in major trouble: 50,000 businesses went **bankrupt**, while others laid off workers to save money, meaning that unemployment rose sharply. There were 1.8 million unemployed at the start of 1929. By January 1932, over 6 million Germans were unemployed – one in three of all workers. Almost every family in Germany faced difficulties in affording food and keeping warm in winter.

### What did the Weimar government do?

The Weimar government could not agree what to do about the Depression.

> If the government spends more, we might have hyperinflation again. We must cut benefits, not increase them. We must raise taxes.

> We *should* increase unemployment benefits for all the unemployed people, but higher taxes to pay for this would hurt big business.

> The SPD refuses to allow tax increases or cuts to benefits. Unemployment benefits must increase.

**DO IT!**

Read this account of the impacts of the Depression on Germany and then answer these questions.

- The Depression in Germany happened because of a banking crisis in the USA. [True / False]

- Germany did not suffer too badly from the Depression because its recovery 1924–29 was built on very firm financial foundations. [True / False]

- Although the working classes suffered from unemployment, other social groups in Germany did not suffer during the Depression. [True / False]

## Election results: September 1930

In Septmeber 1930, the Chancellor decided to call an election as a way of getting support for his policies, however the election results did not help the Weimar Republic one bit. Many more people voted for extreme parties that were against Weimar democracy:

- the Communist Party (KPD) on the extreme left won 23 more seats in the Reichstag
- the Nazi Party (NSDAP) on the extreme right won 95 more seats.

This was the breakthrough election for the Nazi Party.

- In 1928 it was a small party with just 12 seats in the Reichstag. In the 1928 elections the Nazis won 810,000 votes: just 3 per cent of all the votes.
- In the 1930 election the Nazis got 6.4 million votes (18 per cent) and with 107 seats in the Reichstag it was the second largest party after the SPD.

## Why did support for the Nazis increase between 1928 and 1932?

Germans blamed the Weimar government for their suffering in the Depression. Government policies meant higher taxes, wage cuts and higher food prices because of government **tariffs** on imports.

### DO IT!

The initials for the seven reasons (given below) why Nazi support increased between 1928 and 1932 spell MOSFLOP.

1 Come up with a mental image to help you remember MOSFLOP.

2 Can you remember what MOSFLOP stands for, with this book closed?

---

1 **Message:** The Nazis focused on issues that most Germans could identify with: solving Germany's economic problems, reversing the Treaty of Versailles, making Germany great again.

2 **Organisation:** The Nazi Party was very well organised: orders from the top (Hitler) were carried out by enthusiastic party members throughout Germany, and the party was very good at raising money for their campaigns.

3 **Strength:** The Nazis' military strength (the SA) convinced many Germans that they would restore law and order in Germany and prevent a communist uprising.

7 **Propaganda:** Joseph Goebbels organised very effective propaganda for the Nazi Party. The Nazi's used strong, simple messages in their posters, leaflets and radio and film broadcasts, and projected an image of strength and determination with mass rallies and marches.

4 **Fear:** Votes for the KPD (communists) increased in 1928 among working-class Germans, which made many other Germans frightened of a communist takeover. The Nazis looked like the only political party that could stop this.

6 **Opponents:** The Nazis' political opponents were the socialists (SPD) and communists (KPD). But these left-wing groups argued among themselves rather than coming up with effective anti-Nazi messages: opposition was weak.

5 **Leadership:** While the Weimar government looked weak and undecided about how to tackle the Depression, Hitler was a strong leader with a clear plan.

## Role of the SA

Hitler set up the SA (Sturmabteilung – meaning assault division) in 1921. The SA was used to:

- protect Nazi Party speakers at public meetings from disruption by opponents

- disrupt speakers from other political parties at public meetings, tear down opposition posters and intimidate rival candidates in elections

- demonstrate Nazi Party strength and discipline in rallies and marches

- organise the Hitler Youth (until 1932)

- battle the Nazis' opponents in street fights, especially the Red Front Fighters League (RFB), the KPD's version of the SA. One clash in 1932 left 18 dead.

In 1930 the SA had around 100,000 members – this increased to around 400,000 by 1932 and 2 million by January 1933.

## Hitler's appeal

The failure of the Munich Putsch (1923) convinced Hitler that the Nazi Party could not take power by force. Instead it must gain power by winning elections. In order to do this, Hitler understood that he needed to appeal to many different groups of Germans.

**NAILIT!**

The key reasons for the increase in support for the Nazis between 1928 and 1932 are:

- Hitler's appeal

- the impact of the Depression

- the failure of the Weimar government to deal with the Depression.

Hitler's message was always hopeful and encouraging, which appealed to the suffering German people.

The things Hitler promised to do when elected were vague, rather than specific, so people found them difficult to disagree with. The Nazis stood for traditional values, a strong economy and a great Germany.

Hitler presented himself as an ordinary person – he was not a Prussian baron or a rich factory owner.

Hitler hated Jews and blamed them for all Germany's problems. Many Germans were ready to believe this – rather than take any blame for the problems themselves.

**Hitler's appeal**

Germans who had fought in the war could relate to Hitler – he was an infantryman who had won two Iron Cross medals for bravery.

Hitler promised different things to different groups: for example, work for unemployed people but higher profits for big business. This widened his appeal.

He repeated simple slogans and catchphrases that people remembered and related to, such as 'Work and Bread'.

People spoke of being converted by Hitler – like a religious experience. He built up an image of being Germany's saviour.

Hitler was a charismatic, dramatic and 'spellbinding' public speaker, making an emotional connection with his audience.

# Who voted for the Nazis?

## Unemployed workers

The Nazis promised jobs with good wages and good working conditions. However, many workers chose to support the KPD instead of the Nazis because the communists promised to share out all Germany's wealth more equally to benefit the workers.

## Middle classes

Germany's middle classes had lost jobs, savings and pensions in the Depression and blamed the weak Weimar government for their suffering. They believed the Nazi Party would provide the strong leadership that Germany needed. The middle classes were also frightened of a communist uprising, which would take what they had left and give it to the workers. They saw the Nazi Party as strong enough to save Germany from communism.

## Big business

The wealthy owners of Germany's industries were worried about communists because they would take away their factories and their money. The Nazis convinced many industrialists that they were the only party that could stop this. Big business also liked Nazi plans to rebuild Germany's military power – these would mean very valuable contracts for armaments companies like Krupps. Some industrialists donated large amounts of money to the Nazi Party, helping to fund its expensive election campaigns.

## Young people

The Nazis were successful in getting votes from first-time voters. Young people were attracted by Hitler's charisma, the excitement of Nazi rallies and marches, and the promise of being part of something important and meaningful. Over 40 per cent of Nazi Party members in 1930 were under 30 years old.

## Women

Women had the vote and made up 50 per cent of the electorate. By 1930, the Nazis began to target women voters by promising a return to traditional family values. Although the Weimar Republic had given women more freedom and some equality with men, there were many women who opposed this and believed a woman's place was in the home, looking after her children and her husband.

## Farmers

The Nazis were very successful in convincing farmers to vote for them in 1930. The Depression had caused a fall in food prices, which hurt farmers. The Nazis promised to protect farmers from having their farms repossessed and to keep prices for farm goods from falling. Before 1928, most farmers were against the Nazis because Nazi policy was to put all land into national ownership. But in 1928 the Nazis changed this and said only Jews would have their lands confiscated.

## NAIL IT!

There are different points of view on the reasons for the growth in support for the Nazi Party between 1928 and 1932, which makes this topic a good one for interpretation questions. MOSFLOP (see page 26) can help you to evaluate interpretations on this.

# The failure of Weimar democracy

## Impact of the September 1930 election

Chancellor Brüning had called the 1930 election hoping to get more support for his unpopular policies. Instead he got less support because both the Nazi Party and the KPD refused to back his policies.

Chancellor Brüning relied more and more on getting President Hindenburg to pass laws without the Reichstag. For example, in 1932 the Reichstag passed just five laws, while presidential decree was used to pass 66 laws. This meant the government was no longer democratic. Historians agree that this is when the Weimar Republic ended in failure.

## Chancellor Brüning's policies

Chancellor Brüning's policies made things worse after 1930 when he:

- cut wages for government jobs by 23 per cent
- cut unemployment benefits by 60 per cent
- increased tax rates for products like sugar and beer, making prices higher
- introduced new taxes.

The economic and social crisis in Germany escalated:

- In 1931 an important bank went bust and all Germany's banks closed for three weeks. Unemployment rose rapidly: by the start of 1933 over 6 million Germans were unemployed.
- Even those who had still got jobs were suffering because employers cut wages. By 1932 wages were 30 per cent lower than they had been in 1928.
- Street fighting between the SA and the KPD's Red Front Fighters increased. Around 300 people were killed in fighting in 1932, and more than 1000 people were wounded. In April 1932, Brüning wanted to ban the SA to restore order – but his ban was overturned.

In May 1932, President Hindenburg forced Brüning to resign as Chancellor.

## Election results: 1932

There were three elections in 1932: a presidential election and two Reichstag elections.

- Hindenburg won the presidential election with 53 per cent of the vote. Although Hitler lost (he got 37 per cent of the vote), the election campaign had spread Hitler's message throughout Germany. 13.4 million Germans had voted for Hitler to become President.
- The Reichstag election in July 1932 was a massive triumph for the Nazi Party. The Nazi party was now the largest party in the Reichstag.

The Nazi Party result was the largest vote for any one party in Reichstag history – however, it was not a majority of Reichstag seats.

| Reichstag election | NSDAP (Nazi Party) | KPD (communists) | SPD |
|---|---|---|---|
| 1928 | 12 seats 3% of vote | 54 seats 11% of vote | 153 seats 30% of vote |
| 1930 | 107 seats 18% of vote | 77 seats 13% of vote | 143 seats 25% of vote |
| July 1932 | 230 seats 37% of vote | 89 seats 14% of vote | 133 seats 22% of vote |

The KPD increased their seats, though less dramatically. Between them, the Nazis and the KPD held over half the Reichstag seats – and both refused to work with the government.

## DO IT!

Take a picture of the election votes table above. These election results are worth learning by heart.

## Papen and Hindenburg

In May 1932 President Hindenburg forced Chancellor Brüning to resign and appointed Franz von Papen (from the Centre Party). There were three main reasons for this:

**Brüning's failed policies**
Brüning's policies of cutting government spending had made the economic crisis worse, not better.

**Brüning's ban of the SA**
Schleicher, head of the German army, convinced Hindenburg that the SA was needed to stop the communists.

**Brüning's plans for land**
Hindenburg feared that Brüning planned to give away Prussian farmland to the unemployed.

### The rise and fall of Chancellor Papen

Papen wanted to support the rich landowners and industrialists. In 1932:

Papen cut back on the rights of the trade unions, who were trying to improve pay and conditions for working people.

↓

Papen shut down the government of Prussia, which had always supported the Weimar Republic, because he said they were not dealing with security issues.

↓

Papen called a new Reichstag election in November 1932, hoping to get more support for his right-wing policies.

↓

When the November election failed to get Papen more support, Hindenburg sacked Papen in December 1932 and made Schleicher the Chancellor instead.

Franz von Papen

# How did Hitler become Chancellor?

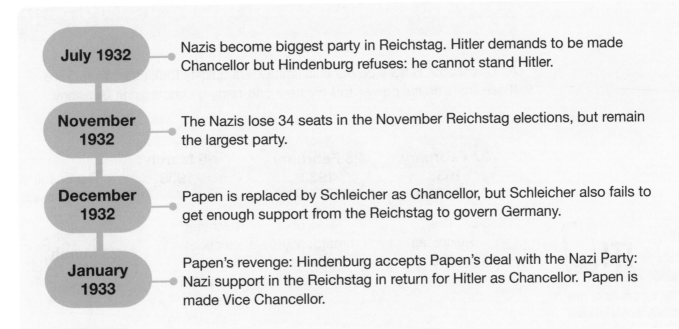

| | |
|---|---|
| **July 1932** | Nazis become biggest party in Reichstag. Hitler demands to be made Chancellor but Hindenburg refuses: he cannot stand Hitler. |
| **November 1932** | The Nazis lose 34 seats in the November Reichstag elections, but remain the largest party. |
| **December 1932** | Papen is replaced by Schleicher as Chancellor, but Schleicher also fails to get enough support from the Reichstag to govern Germany. |
| **January 1933** | Papen's revenge: Hindenburg accepts Papen's deal with the Nazi Party: Nazi support in the Reichstag in return for Hitler as Chancellor. Papen is made Vice Chancellor. |

## Papen's revenge!

Papen was furious with Schleicher for persuading Hindenburg to sack him. When Schleicher also failed to get enough support from the Reichstag to pass laws, Papen saw his chance for revenge.

> Papen convinced Hindenburg that a deal with the Nazi Party would solve their problems. If Hindenburg made Hitler the Chancellor, the government would have the support of the Nazis – the largest party in the Reichstag. That way the government would have the votes in the Reichstag they required to make the changes Germany needed. It was true, Papen said, that the Nazi Party was backed by violent thugs and had unrealistic and unpleasant policies, but between them, Hindenburg and Papen were sure they could make Hitler do what they wanted. Papen would be Vice Chancellor, controlling Hitler behind the scenes. Papen said he had Hitler 'in his pocket'.

**DO IT!**

Read the account above and answer the following questions:

1 'This account suggests that Hitler became Chancellor because of political deal-making.' Do you agree with this statement or not? Add one piece of evidence from the interpretation to back up your answer.

2 'In my view, this account is not very useful because it does not consider the reasons why Hitler was so popular in Germany.' Do you agree with this statement or not? Add one piece of evidence from your own knowledge to back up your answer.

# The establishment of Hitler's dictatorship

As Chancellor, Hitler's power was limited. He quickly took steps to remove these limits on his power and create a one-party dictatorship in Germany.

Take a photo of this timeline. Make up a song, poem or rap to help you remember it. For example, it could start: 'In February of '33, Hitler claimed a state of emergency / He said a fire at the Reichstag building / was the start of a communist uprising'.

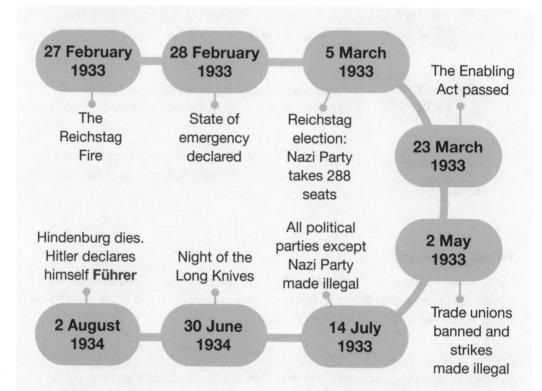

**27 February 1933** — The Reichstag Fire

**28 February 1933** — State of emergency declared

**5 March 1933** — Reichstag election: Nazi Party takes 288 seats

The Enabling Act passed

**23 March 1933**

**2 May 1933** — Trade unions banned and strikes made illegal

**14 July 1933** — All political parties except Nazi Party made illegal

**30 June 1934** — Night of the Long Knives

**2 August 1934** — Hindenburg dies. Hitler declares himself **Führer**

## The Reichstag Fire (27 February 1933)

| **Summary** Hitler used the Reichstag Fire to: | The Reichstag building was destroyed by a fire. Police caught a young Dutch communist called Marinus van der Lubbe in the building. |
| --- | --- |
| • claim a communist uprising was happening | Van der Lubbe said he was acting alone. Whether this was true or not, the Nazi leadership said the fire was the start of a communist uprising. Hitler vowed to crush the communists 'with an iron fist'. |
| • use his communist scare story to push Hindenburg into granting his government emergency powers | Overnight, 4000 communists were rounded up by the police and imprisoned. |
| | The next day, Hitler convinced Hindenburg to declare a state of emergency. This gave the government powers to arrest people, imprison them without trial, search houses, listen in on telephone calls and read private letters. |
| • weaken communist opponents with arrests. | None of these actions broke any laws – in fact, the President had ruled by decree on several occasions already during the Weimar Republic. |

## Reichstag elections (5 March 1933)

- The Nazi Party won 44 per cent of the vote and 288 seats in the Reichstag.

- This meant Hitler still did not have the two-thirds majority of the Reichstag that he needed to overturn the **constitution**. The SPD and Centre Party held onto their seats and would block him.

- Although Hitler said the result showed huge support for Nazi policies, in fact more Germans voted for other parties than for the Nazis in 1933.

- Days of rioting followed this election, as Nazis attacked Jewish-owned shops and people associated with opposition to the Nazi Party.

Describe why the March 1933 elections might have disappointed Hitler, even though in public he said they were a triumph?

## The Enabling Act (24 March 1933)

**Summary**

The Enabling Act meant that for four years Hitler could pass laws without having to get the Reichstag or the President to agree them.

The Enabling Act gave Hitler the power to create a dictatorship. Democracy ended.

The Enabling Act gave Hitler's cabinet the power to pass decrees (laws) that Hitler put forward without either the Reichstag or the President needing to agree them first.

The Reichstag passed the Enabling Act by 444 votes to 94 – well over the two-thirds majority needed. How did Hitler persuade other parties to give away their powers?

One way Hitler got the Reichstag to pass the Enabling Act was the ban on the KPD after the Reichstag fire: 81 KPD deputies and another 26 socialist deputies were prevented from voting in the Enabling Act.

A second way was to use the SA to intimidate deputies into voting for the Enabling Act. Only the SPD voted against the Act.

A third way was to do deals with parties to get them to co-operate. The Centre Party agreed to vote for the Enabling Act in return for being allowed to keep control over Catholic schools.

Hitler got these powers legally, without breaking the law. The Enabling Act was renewed in 1937.

**STRETCH IT!**

Research how Hitler removed possible opposition from regional government and the civil service.

Imagine you are an ordinary German in 1933. Would you have agreed that the Enabling Act was necessary, or would you have opposed it? Write your view in a sentence.

## Elimination of the opposition

Hitler used his new Enabling Act powers to remove possible political opponents to his rule.

| Possible opponents | Why a problem for Hitler's dictatorship? | How was the problem eliminated? |
|---|---|---|
| **Trade unions** | Trade unions were socialist organisations and might organise strikes against Hitler's government, which would limit his power to govern Germany as he thought best. | On 2 May 1933, the SA and SS broke into trade union offices and arrested trade union leaders. |
| | | Hitler used his Enabling Act powers to made trade unions illegal and to ban strikes. |
| | | The German Labour Front (DAF) was set up instead to manage all issues of workers' rights and wages. All workers had to join the DAF. |
| **Political parties** | Hitler was opposed to democracy and did not want any other political party influencing what German people thought or organising opposition to his rule. | The KPD was banned after the Reichstag fire and all its property confiscated. |
| | | On 10 May the SA took over SPD offices. The SPD was then officially banned on 22 June 1933. |
| | | Over June and July the other political parties agreed to shut themselves down. |
| | | On 14 July the Nazi Party was declared the only legal political party in Germany. |

**DO IT!**

Take a photo of the diagram above. Take a break and then write notes on the problems facing Hitler's dictatorship in 1933, and how those problems were eliminated.

## The Night of the Long Knives (30 June 1934)

In the Night of the Long Knives, the main leaders of the SA were shot by members of the SS, supported by the army. Around 100 SA leaders were murdered, with no resistance. Following this, the SA were mostly disarmed: their role was then mainly to take part in rallies. The SS became the force that the Nazis used for political control within Germany.

### Why was the SA a threat?

This photo shows members of the SA in 1933. By 1933 there were 3 million SA members: enough to take control of Germany for themselves.

The leader of the SA was Ernst Röhm. He wanted the army and the SA to be joined together, with him in overall control.

Many SA members were young, working-class men. They were often anti-elite; they did not think big business and wealthy upper-class people should continue to have a better life in Nazi Germany than working people.

### Why did Hitler order the Night of the Long Knives?

- The army hated the idea of a merger with the 'thugs' of the SA and their openly gay leader, Röhm. Hitler needed the support of the army – the army could overthrow his government, and he needed them for his plans for Germany.

- Big business and the wealthy upper classes were worried by the SA's violence and their calls for a more socialist 'second revolution'. Hitler needed big business and wealthy Germans to back his plans for Germany.

- Other Nazi leaders, such as Himmler and Göring, wanted more power for themselves and persuaded Hitler that Röhm was planning to overthrow him.

## Hitler becomes Führer (2 August 1934)

Hindenburg died on 2 August 1934. Hitler announced that the powers of the President were now joined with the powers of the Chancellor in a new role: the Führer. The army was now required to swear an oath of loyalty to the Führer.

## DO IT!

1 With this book closed, write down the main steps in the creation of Hitler's dictatorship, from Reichstag Fire to Führer.

2 Which of the steps in the creation of Hitler's dictatorship do you think was the most important? Explain why.

# CHECKIT! ✓

1 What were the seven major reasons (MOSFLOP) explaining the growth in support for the Nazi Party?

2 Explain why the Depression increased support for extremist parties.

3 How many Reichstag seats did the Nazi Party win in:
 a September 1930
 b July 1932
 c November 1932?

4 What event happened on 27 February 1933 and why was it significant?

5 What event happened on 24 March 1933 and why was it significant?

6 What event happened on 30 June 1934 and why was it significant?

# Part Three:
## The experiences of Germans under the Nazis

## Economic changes

**DO IT!**

Explain how:
- rearmament created jobs
- conscription reduced unemployment
- policies for women created jobs for men.

### Employment

One of Hitler's main priorities was to reduce unemployment in Germany, for example he had promised in the 1933 election to abolish unemployment. The Nazi state was successful in achieving this. The number of unemployed people fell from 4.8 million in 1933 to 0.3 million in 1939. However, there were drawbacks: living conditions did not improve quickly for German workers because the Nazi state kept a strict control on wages through the DAF, which replaced trade unions (see page 34).

**Public works** – the state building projects (e.g. **autobahns**) created new jobs.

**Rearmament** – government contracts boosted military production, creating jobs.

**National Labour Service** – all young men served six months in the NLS.

**Conscription** – for all young men from 1935.

**Creating demand** – Germans were encouraged to buy cars, which were tax free.

**How was unemployment reduced?**

**Controls on employers** – employers needed government permission before they reduced numbers of workers.

**Women** – from 1933, women were barred from some jobs and **propaganda** encouraged them to stay at home. By 1934, 360,000 women had left their jobs.

**Jews** – from 1933, Jews were banned from government jobs.

**Prisons** – by 1939, 160,000 people were in prison for 'crimes' against the Nazi state.

**Statistics** – from 1935 the government counted all part-time workers as full-time.

**STRETCH IT!**

Historians say some Nazi policies 'hid' unemployment rather than creating new jobs. Which policies on the diagram below do you think did this?

Road construction in Nazi Germany.

## Public works programmes

Public works programmes were large-scale projects that benefited the public and which the government paid for. Government spending increased by 70 per cent between 1933 and 1936.

| Examples of public works programmes | Building autobahns (motorway networks), hospitals, housing estates, railway extensions. |
| --- | --- |
| How did this reduce unemployment? | These state-funded projects created millions of jobs. For example, the autobahn programme created 125,000 jobs by 1935. By 1936, two million Germans were working on construction projects. |

The National Labour Service (RAD) meant all young men (18–25) were given work to do.

| Examples of RAD projects | RAD members worked on public work programmes, military projects and conservation projects, e.g. planting and repairing river banks. |
| --- | --- |
| How did this reduce unemployment? | From 1935 it was compulsory for all 18-year-old men to spend six months in the RAD before going into the army. There were 422,000 people in the RAD in 1935, all counted as employed. |

## Rearmament

Hitler wanted to rebuild Germany's military power so that the country would be ready for war; this is known as rearmament. The amount the government spent on rearmament increased from 3.5 billion marks in 1933 to 26 billion marks by 1939. Rearmament also reduced unemployment.

| Examples of rearmament projects | Increasing production of weapons, military equipment, uniforms. Conscription was introduced for the German army in 1935: at age 19 all young men went into the army for two years. |
| --- | --- |
| How did this reduce unemployment? | German businesses expanded as they increased production, creating millions of jobs. As a result of conscription by 1939 there were 1.3 million men 'employed' in the German armed forces. |

### Employment: benefits and drawbacks

**Benefits:**

✓ By 1939, there was almost full employment in Germany: it was actually difficult for some employers to find workers.

**Drawbacks:**

✗ Not all young people enjoyed labour service: the pay was low, the work was hard (up to 76 hours a week) and the living conditions were basic.

✗ Strict controls on wages by the German Labour Front (DAF) meant that although people had jobs, they did not feel they were getting richer.

## Self-sufficiency

By 1934 the German economy was facing problems.

More people in jobs meant people wanted to buy more things, but there were shortages. For example, German farmers were not producing enough butter.

Many more German factories were now producing for rearmament. However, Germany could not produce all the **raw materials** needed for rearmament. Nor were German factories producing as much to export to other countries.

The result was that Germany was spending more on **imports** (raw materials, food products) and was not earning enough from its exports to pay for them.

### — Guns or butter? —

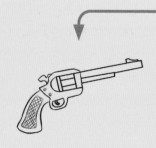

By 1936, rearmament was slowing down as German factories ran out of raw materials. Economic experts said Germany could have 'guns or butter'. That meant Hitler must either prioritise rearmament and introduce food rationing, or reduce rearmament and prioritise producing exports.

Hitler rejected this and demanded both rearmament and enough food to feed the German people without **rationing**. A new Four Year Plan was introduced in 1936 to achieve this, headed by Göring. The aims of the plan were to:

- make Germany **self-sufficient** in raw materials, especially the rubber, oil and metals that it was currently importing

- increase food production.

One way that Göring planned to meet these targets was to find ways to make the raw materials Germany needed from other things. These were called **ersatz** goods. For example, German scientists worked out a way of making petrol from coal. However, the Four Year Plan failed to make Germany self-sufficient. Germany was still importing 33 per cent of its raw materials and 20 per cent of its food in 1939.

Explain how life in Germany would have changed for the following three men as a result of economic changes brought in by the Nazis after 1933?

- A factory worker, unemployed since 1930
- An 18-year-old student
- The owner of a factory

**STRETCHIT!**

Do you think the Nazis' economic policies had more benefits than drawbacks for the German people, or the other way around? Back up your views with evidence.

## The impact of war

The Second World War began in September 1939 when Germany invaded Poland. By 1940, Germany had invaded six more European countries, including France. Next, Hitler planned to defeat the Soviet Union. His invasion began very well in 1941, but by the start of 1943 the Soviet Union was winning. In June 1944, Britain and the USA invaded France, then Germany, and in May 1945 the German army surrendered.

### Bombing

Over 300,000 Germans were killed by Allied bombing and 3.6 million homes were destroyed: one-fifth of all Germany's housing. The bombing campaigns aimed to weaken German morale as well as to damage Germany's economy.

- In some areas that were bombed very often, Germans did find it difficult to keep going, but generally Germans continued to believe Germany would win the war right up to the very end of the conflict.

- The bombing created thousands of **refugees**: those made homeless and those looking for safer places to live (for example, the Ruhr was bombed day and night).

- Critics of the Allied bombing said that it had not been effective because the Germans had managed to increase their production of aircraft, tanks, weapons and ammunition. However, Germany did not increase production by as much as countries such as Britain, the USA and the USSR did. This was probably due to the bombing.

### Rationing

Germans remembered the terrible food shortages at the end of the First World War, which had led to revolution. To prevent this happening again, the Nazi state introduced rationing of some food products in 1939, from the very start of the war. Conquering France brought more food into Germany, but from 1942 rations had to be reduced for food, household products (e.g. soap) and clothes. Although rationing made life difficult for Germans, it did prevent the severe shortages of 1918. Only in 1945 did Germans experience real hunger.

### Labour shortages

By 1940, 3.5 million men had joined the armed forces, followed by another 1.7 million in 1941 and another 1.4 million in 1942. This caused major labour shortages in Germany – there were simply not enough workers. The Nazi state tried to solve these labour shortages in two main ways:

- They brought in workers from the countries they had defeated. For example, by the end of 1942, 6.4 million foreign workers were being forced to work in Germany, often in very bad conditions. By the end of the war, the number of foreign workers in Germany was over 8 million. However, foreign workers did as little work as they could get away with, so this did not solve the labour problem.

- They made production methods more efficient. This worked very well, despite labour shortages and damage done by bombing. For example, production of all weapons increased by 130 per cent between 1941 and 1943.

**DOIT!**

Imagine you are a 16-year-old living in Germany in 1943. How is your life affected by the war? Try to describe your hopes and fears as well as the practical changes to how you live.

**NAILIT!**

There will always be a question on how the lives of the German people, or specific groups of German people (e.g. young people), changed during a period. Think about how lives changed as a result of the war when you revise this section.

# Social policy and practice

## How did Nazi policies affect women?

The Nazis believed in traditional values for men and women: women's role was to marry, have children and look after the family home.

**Women sacked from state jobs**

Women in government jobs were dismissed and replaced by men.

**Propaganda**

The state encouraged its traditional values through newspaper and magazine articles, radio and film, posters and leaflets.

DIE NSDAP SICHERT DIE VOLKS-GEMEINSCHAFT

VOLKSGENOSSEN BRAUCHT IHR RAT UND HILFE SO WENDET EUCH AN DIE ORTSGRUPPE

**Loans to encourage marriage**

The government gave newly-weds 1000 marks as a loan. The more children the couple went on to have, the less they had to pay back. However, the woman had to leave her job to get the loan.

**Nazi policies and women**

**Medals for babies**

The state gave medals to mothers who had a lot of children: four children = bronze, six = silver, and eight = gold.

**Impact of policies**

- Nazi policies on marriage and babies worked: the number of marriages and the number of babies increased. For example, there were around 200,000 more marriages as a result of Nazi policies.

- Nazi policies on women staying at home were less effective: the number of women working actually increased by 2.4 million between 1933 and 1939. This was linked to shortages of male workers as more and more men went into the army.

## How did Nazi policies affect young people?

Hitler wanted German young people to be brought up believing in Nazi ideals and his leadership. Nazi youth groups and Nazi education policies were designed to do this.

### The Hitler Youth and the League of German Maidens (BDM)

Everyone who joined the Hitler Youth swore an oath to Adolf Hitler. They promised to put Hitler first in everything in their lives.

The League of German Maidens was the girls' part of the Hitler Youth. Both boys and girls did a lot of PE in the Hitler Youth, but while boys also did military training, girls learned how to be housewives.

**Nazi policies and young people**

### Education

School subjects delivered Nazi ideology, for example:

- biology lessons included Nazi racial ideas about the superiority of the **Aryan race**

- the amount of PE in the school timetable was doubled

- boys and girls had some different subjects, for example girls did domestic science: cooking and sewing.

### Impact of policies

- In 1939, 80 per cent of young people were in the Hitler Youth because in March 1939 it became compulsory to join. Before then, many chose not to join: 4 million were in the Hitler Youth in 1936 – almost 5 million fewer than in 1939.

- There is evidence that while young people liked the sports, many found the lectures on Nazi ideology boring. Others did become loyal, committed Nazis, however.

### Nazi control of education

The Nazi state was very successful at controlling education. It did this by controlling teachers. By 1937, 97 per cent of teachers had joined the National Socialist Teachers' League. Many had joined willingly: in 1934, 25 per cent of teachers were already Nazi Party members, compared to 10 per cent of all Germans.

- Teachers hoped that supporting the Nazis would improve their wages and give teaching higher status in German society.

- In fact, Nazi policies did not help teachers. Pay did not increase, teachers were made to teach Nazi propaganda instead of teaching their subjects properly, and students were encouraged by the Hitler Youth to challenge teachers and even mock them.

## STRETCHIT!

Find out about Martin Niemöller and his opposition to Nazi control of churches and religion.

## Nazi control of churches and religion

The Nazi view of Christianity was that it made Germans weak and that it had Jewish roots. Hitler did not want religious leaders to influence what Germans thought, only him. However, most Germans were Christians: either Protestant (two-thirds of Germans) or Catholic (one-third). Attacking the Church directly would upset too many Germans.

**Nazi control of churches and religion**

The Catholic and Protestant Churches were worried about the spread of communism, which wanted to get rid of religion completely.

The Nazis seemed the only party that could protect Germany and the Churches from communism.

The **Catholic Church** did a deal with the Nazi state in 1933 called a **concordat.**

The **Protestant Church** in Germany was taken over by Nazis from the inside.

In return for a promise from the Church to stay out of politics and Catholic bishops swearing an oath of loyalty to Hitler, the Nazis said the Catholic Church would stay independent.

A Nazi called Ludwig Muller became the 'Reich Bishop' of the Church and this part of the Protestant Church gave the Nazis their support.

However...

However...

The Nazis did not keep their promise. In 1936, Catholic youth groups were forced to join the Hitler Youth and the state began to shut down Catholic monasteries and nunneries.

Some German Protestants set up a new church called the Confessing Church. This church opposed the Nazis and many of its members were arrested.

## DOIT!

Explain the reasons why the Nazis wanted to control women, young people and religious people. Do these reasons have anything in common?

How successful do you think the Nazis' social policies were in controlling women, young people and religious people? Back up your answer with some evidence.

## Racial policy and persecution

The Nazis believed that the German race belonged to a 'master race' that was better than all others: the Aryans. They wanted to exclude from Germany any people they saw as 'inferior' who they believed they would 'weaken' the 'master race'. 'Inferior' people included:

- people the Nazis believed didn't 'fit in' to society, such as gay men – tens of thousands were sent to **concentration camps;** many died there

- people with physical and mental disabilities – people with these conditions were often sterilized (from 1933), which meant they could not have children of their own; from 1939, the Nazis murdered thousands of disabled children and adults

- people the Nazis classified as 'inferior races', especially gypsies and Jews – the Nazis were obsessively anti-Semitic, blaming Jews for every problem that Germany had.

### Persecution of Jews

The Nazi Party's **persecution** of German Jews began in 1933.

### The Final Solution

- In the war the Nazi persecution of Jews spread to countries occupied by Germany, for example Poland. Jews were forced from their homes and made to live in ghettos, where many starved to death or died of disease.

**1933** — Many German Jews with government jobs (e.g. civil service) were sacked.

**1935** — The Nuremburg Laws:

- Jews could no longer be citizens of Germany. They had no rights to vote, for example.

- Jews were not allowed to marry or have sexual relationships with German citizens.

**1938** — Kristallnacht (9 November): Hitler approved a night of terror against Jews, following the assassination of a German diplomat in Paris by a Jew.

- 91 Jews were murdered, 7000 Jewish businesses and 177 synagogues were destroyed. 20,000 Jews were sent to concentration camps.

- Jews were forbidden from running businesses or employing workers.

- Jewish children could no longer go to 'Aryan' schools.

**1939** — The Reich Office for Jewish Emigration was set up, forcing all Jews to **emigrate** from Germany.

**1939: 30 April** — German Jews were forced to leave their homes and live in Jewish-only **ghettos**.

**1941** — All Jews in Germany had to wear the **Star of David** on their clothes.

- When Germany attacked the USSR in 1941, it gained control over areas in which 3 million Jews lived. SS units began killing thousands of Jews in eastern Europe in mass shootings.

- In January 1942, a group of senior Nazis met to discuss a 'Final Solution' to kill all the Jews of Europe. The head of the SS and **Gestapo**, Himmler, organised a system of death camps and labour camps where Jews and other 'inferior' people were murdered with gas, shot or worked to death.

- Six million Jews and 500,000 gypsies were murdered in the 'Final Solution'. Hundreds of thousands of others were also killed because they came from groups that the Nazis discriminated against.

**NAILIT!**

Learn the stages (and their dates) by which persecution of Jews intensified under the Nazi regime. Using this information accurately and relevantly will boost marks.

# Control

## How did the Nazis use propaganda and censorship?

Joseph Goebbels was in charge of the Ministry of Propaganda. He had total control over Nazi culture. Earlier, Goebbels had been responsible for propaganda in the Nazi election campaigns of 1930 and 1933.

Goebbels' Ministry of Propaganda told journalists what to write and how to write it. The Nazis also bought up newspapers so they could control them directly. By 1939, the Nazis owned 69 per cent of all Germany's newspapers.

Goebbels was also in charge of **censorship**: making sure nothing that criticised the Nazis appeared in any newspaper or book, or in any film, play or radio broadcast, etc. Instead, these media should all praise the Nazis and, especially, Hitler.

Radio broadcasts were very important for Nazi propaganda. Hitler understood that he could talk to people directly with a radio broadcast. Production of cheap radios increased under the Nazis, so that by 1939, 70 per cent of German families owned a radio.

Propaganda encouraged Germans to behave in certain ways. For example, people were expected to greet each other with the 'Heil Hitler' salute. Apartment blocks were expected to display Nazi banners and flags during marches.

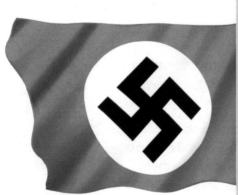

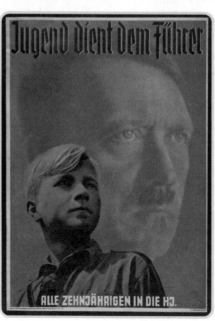

Propaganda posters were widely used to promote Hitler and the Nazi Party.

## Nazi culture

In 1933 the Reich Chamber of Culture was set up, as part of the Ministry of Propaganda. Its job was to make sure that all different kinds of cultural activity in Germany promoted Nazi values.

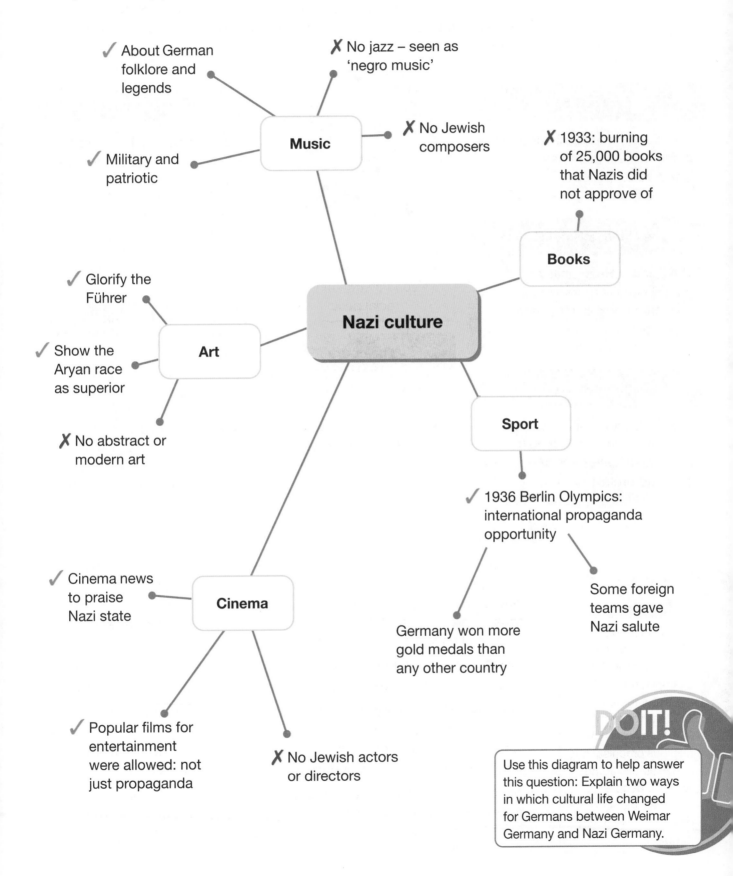

✓ About German folklore and legends

✗ No jazz – seen as 'negro music'

✗ No Jewish composers

**Music**

✓ Military and patriotic

✗ 1933: burning of 25,000 books that Nazis did not approve of

**Books**

✓ Glorify the Führer

✓ Show the Aryan race as superior

**Art**

✗ No abstract or modern art

**Nazi culture**

**Sport**

✓ 1936 Berlin Olympics: international propaganda opportunity

Some foreign teams gave Nazi salute

Germany won more gold medals than any other country

✓ Cinema news to praise Nazi state

**Cinema**

✓ Popular films for entertainment were allowed: not just propaganda

✗ No Jewish actors or directors

**DOIT!**

Use this diagram to help answer this question: Explain two ways in which cultural life changed for Germans between Weimar Germany and Nazi Germany.

## The Nazi police state

The Nazi state was a police state: the Nazis had complete control over the police and used them to control the German people without there being any limits on state powers. This meant the police did not need evidence to lock people up, and people accused of crimes had no hope of a fair trial.

The head of the Nazi police state was Heinrich Himmler, who answered only to Hitler himself.

### The SS

The SS combatted all opposition to the Nazis and enforced the Nazis' racial policies.

### The Death's Heads Units

The Death's Head units of the SS were responsible for concentration camps and the Final Solution.

### Concentration camps

The first concentration camps were set up in 1933. Conditions were harsh, with hard labour, little food and brutal punishments.

Himmler was the head of the SS, the Gestapo and the state police. He was also in charge of Nazi racial policy.

### The courts

Judges and the court system were controlled by the Nazis. People accused of anti-Nazi crimes were usually found guilty – even if they weren't.

### The state police

Senior positions in Germany's regular police force went to important Nazis, who reported directly to Himmler. The police kept law and order but also looked for possible opposition to the Nazi state.

### The Gestapo

The Gestapo were the Nazis' secret police. They did not wear uniforms. Their role was to search out opposition to the Nazis. They had a lot of power – they could arrest people without evidence and send them to camps without a trial.

## Repression

Hundreds of thousands of Germans were arrested for opposition to the Nazi state. For example, in 1939, 160,000 people were arrested for 'political offences'. However, there were only ever around 30,000 Gestapo officers in Germany, in a country of 80 million people. This meant Nazi **repression** was often based on fear *of* the Gestapo.

- The Gestapo did not wear uniforms so Germans could not tell how many people in their town worked for the Gestapo or if someone was Gestapo.

- The Gestapo used terror to get the results they needed: arrests usually happened early in the morning, waking up the whole apartment block. They were allowed to use torture to get confessions. They could arrest anyone and people who were arrested were sometimes never seen again.

- Most Gestapo arrests were because one member of the public had informed on someone they knew. Many people did this because they were afraid they would be arrested themselves if they failed to pass on the information.

Collect examples of Nazi repression from this book. For example, how did the Nazis repress political opponents (e.g. Communists), religious organisations (e.g. Catholic youth groups), people the Nazis thought didn't 'fit in' (e.g. gay people)?

## Opposition and resistance

It was very dangerous to show any opposition to Nazi control, which makes it difficult to know how far ordinary German people supported the Nazi state. The Nazis became popular because they reduced unemployment and had electoral success, but it appears that many ordinary Germans probably 'went along' with the regime rather than fanatically supporting it.

There were groups of Germans who organised opposition to the Nazi regime. The most serious opposition happened during the war and it was repressed harshly by the Gestapo.

### Opposition by young people

#### The Edelweiss Pirates

Edelweiss Pirates were mainly from industrial cities. They hated the strict military control of the Hitler Youth and dressed in ways to express freedom, such as wearing American-style clothes and longer hair for boys.

Before the war the Pirates sang songs mocking the Hitler Youth, painted anti-Nazi graffiti and occasionally fought Hitler Youth groups. During the war, Edelweiss Pirates help spread Allied anti-Nazi propaganda and looked after deserters from the German army.

In 1944, 13 young people, including Edelweiss Pirates, were hanged on Himmler's orders.

#### The Swing Youth

These were young people from wealthier backgrounds who listened to American 'swing' music (the Nazis hated this 'degenerate' music) and dressed in American fashions.

Over time, the Swing Youth started to organise illegal large-scale dances, involving thousands of young people.

#### The White Rose group

This was a group of students and a university teacher who organised anti-Nazi leaflets and graffiti in Munich during 1942 and 1943. These leaflets included criticism of Jewish persecution.

The Gestapo arrested group members in 1943 and many were executed.

### Opposition from within the Army: July 1944

**The July 1944 bomb plot**

This was a failed attempt to assassinate Hitler with a bomb placed under a meeting table. Some of those involved opposed Jewish persecution. However, the main reason for the plot was that members of the German army no longer trusted Hitler: Germany was facing defeat and Hitler was behaving more and more strangely.

# CHECK IT! ✓

1. Identify two methods the Nazi state used to reduce unemployment.

2. Explain one benefit and one drawback of Nazi employment policies.

3. What did newly-wed women have to do to get the Nazi's 100-mark loan?

4. What was the name (in English) of the Nazi youth organisation for girls?

5. German Jews lost their citizenship as a result of which laws in 1935?

6. Name one group opposed to the Nazis.

# How to answer the exam questions

## Question 1

### About the question

 How does **Interpretation B** differ from **Interpretation A** about…

In this question you compare two interpretations and identify and explain differences between them in terms of their content.

### Answering the question

> 1 Read **Interpretations A** and **B**.
>
> How does **Interpretation B** differ from **Interpretation A** about the reasons for Hitler's appointment as Chancellor?
>
> Explain your answer using **Interpretations A** and **B**.
>
> **(4 marks)**

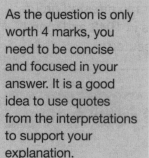

**NAIL**IT!

As the question is only worth 4 marks, you need to be concise and focused in your answer. It is a good idea to use quotes from the interpretations to support your explanation.

---

**Interpretation A**
From the memoirs of a close friend of Hitler, written in 1946.

The author of Interpretation A worked closely with Hitler in the years 1929 to 1933 as an economist and administrator of the SA. He wrote his memoirs while in a military prison after the war.

Hitler had every right to be Chancellor. If the 1930 election had been our breakthrough, then the election of July 1932 proved once and for all that the German people wholeheartedly supported NSDAP policies and yearned to have Hitler lead Germany out of the sorry mess caused by the weak-willed fools of the Weimar Republic. Only Hitler had the answers to make Germany great again and it was his destiny to become our Führer.

**Interpretation B**
From an article written in a British newspaper in 1950. The author had been a British diplomat working in Berlin in 1933.

Papen convinced Hindenburg that a deal with the Nazi Party would solve their problems. If Hindenburg made Hitler the Chancellor, the government would have the support of the largest party in the Reichstag. It was true that the Nazi Party was backed by violent thugs and had unrealistic and unpleasant policies. But between them, Hindenburg and Papen were sure that they could make Hitler do what they wanted. Papen would be Vice Chancellor, controlling Hitler behind the scenes. Papen said he had Hitler 'in his pocket'.

Which of the following options best describes the difference between Interpretations A and B on page 48?

**A** Interpretation A considers the Depression to be the main reason why Hitler became Chancellor.

**B** Interpretation A is more useful because it was written by someone that knew Hitler well.

**C** Interpretation A considers Hitler to have become Chancellor because no one else wanted the job, while Interpretation B says that Hitler became Chancellor by mistake.

**D** Interpretation A sees the Nazi Party's election successes as the reason why Hitler had to be made Chancellor, while Interpretation B suggests Hitler became Chancellor because of Papen's scheming.

It is important to explain your answer to Question 1.

Here are four extracts from student answers to the question using different interpretations: some identify a difference and some explain a difference. (The interpretations are not provided – you don't need them for this activity!)

---

**NAIL**IT!

Level 1 answers (1–2 marks) identify a relevant difference or differences between the interpretations.
Level 2 answers (3–4 marks) explain the difference.

---

**1** A and B are different because Interpretation A is all about Wilhelm's personality being the problem. For example, 'his attention span was short and he did not work hard'. B, however, is about Germany's rapid industrialisation being the reason why Germany was difficult to rule.

**2** A says that hyperinflation was the main problem facing the Weimar Republic because people 'never forgot' it. B says the main problem was the government accepted the Treaty of Versailles. So the interpretations suggest different main problems for the Weimar government.

**3** Interpretation A says that the Naz is set up the Reichstag Fire to look like the communists were responsible, because they wanted an excuse to declare an emergency. But B says that in fact Hitler was sure the Reichstag Fire really was the start of a communist uprising, because they had been expecting one to happen.

**4** A views the Nazi regime's economic policies as being a big success because they reduced unemployment from six million in 1933 to less than one million. However, while A is positive, B is more negative - it says the policies actually caused major long-term economic problems, because Germany started to experience shortages.

---

**DO**IT!

**1** Which of the four student answers to the left do you think are *explaining* the difference rather than just identifying a difference?

**2** Which of the following words or phrases do you think 'signals' to an examiner that *explaining* is happening?

   **A** in fact
   **B** because
   **C** suggest
   **D** says that

---

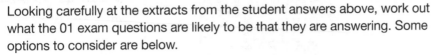

**STRETCH**IT!

Looking carefully at the extracts from the student answers above, work out what the 01 exam questions are likely to be that they are answering. Some options to consider are below.

   **A** How does Interpretation B differ from Interpretation A about the lives of young people in Nazi Germany?
   **B** How does Interpretation B differ from Interpretation A about responsibility for the Reichstag Fire?
   **C** How does Interpretation B differ from Interpretation A about the success of the Nazis' economic policies?
   **D** How does Interpretation B differ from Interpretation A about the problems facing Weimar governments?
   **E** How does Interpretation B differ from Interpretation A about difficulties faced by Kaiser Wilhelm II's governments?

## Question 2

### About the question

Why might the authors of Interpretation A and B have a different interpretation about...

In this question you will need to identify and explain reasons for the difference in the interpretations. You do this by analysing the provenance of the interpretations. There are 4 marks for this question, and you should spend no more than about five minutes on it.

### Answering the question

There are different ways of thinking about provenance. Here are a few options:

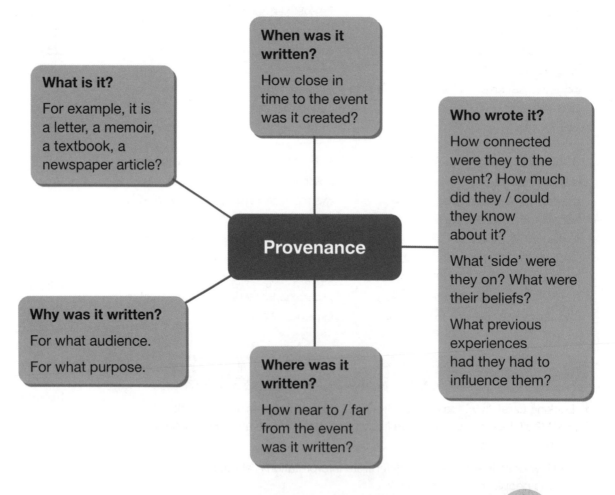

**What is it?**
For example, it is a letter, a memoir, a textbook, a newspaper article?

**When was it written?**
How close in time to the event was it created?

**Who wrote it?**
How connected were they to the event? How much did they / could they know about it?

What 'side' were they on? What were their beliefs?

What previous experiences had they had to influence them?

**Provenance**

**Why was it written?**
For what audience.
For what purpose.

**Where was it written?**
How near to / far from the event was it written?

**NAILIT!**

It isn't possible to know for sure why the authors have different interpretations, which is why it is a good idea to use phrases like 'this suggests that...' or 'this might be because...'

DO IT!

Read the five answers A–E on this page and decide what reason (or reasons) from the provenance diagram has been suggested in each one. The first one has been done for you.

**Student answer A**

Interpretation A was written by a minister in the Nazi government, which means he is likely to see his government's economic policies in a positive way.

*The reason suggested in student answer A = Who wrote it? What side were they on?*

**Student answer B**

Interpretation B was written a long time after the events it is describing, which could mean it is able to consider more factors.

**Student answer C**

Interpretation B is a biography of Kaiser Wilhelm II, which might mean it focuses on the Kaiser rather than considering other factors.

**Student answer D**

Interpretation A was written by a British journalist who had been arrested in Germany because of his support for the Communist Party; this might explain its negative view.

**Student answer E**

Interpretation A was written in the 1930s in the USA, which might explain why it does not consider the Depression to have been as serious for Germany as for the USA.

Read this example exam-style question and the answer that follows it. This question uses the Interpretations A and B on page 48.

**2** Why might the authors of **Interpretations A** and **B** have a different interpretation about the reasons for Hitler's appointment as Chancellor?

Explain your answer using **Interpretations A** and **B** and your contextual knowledge.

**(4 marks)**

## DO IT!

Read the statements about this answer. Tick a statement below if you agree with it and put a cross next to it if you do not think it applies to this answer.

Interpretation A is different from Interpretation B because Interpretation A was written by a close friend of Hitler, so his interpretation will be really positive about Hitler. He also wrote Interpretation B when he was in prison, so he might have been angry about Germany being defeated.

Interpretation B was written by someone who was British. He was in Berlin in 1933 but he probably wasn't really involved in what happened. He wrote his interpretation after the war, when everyone knew that Hitler and the Nazis were evil.

⬜ **a** A good point is that the student wrote about more than one reason why the interpretations might be different.

⬜ **b** A problem with the answer is that the student has not explained why the reasons might have affected the interpretations.

⬜ **c** A good point about the answer is that the student has considered why both interpretations were written: what their purpose and audience were.

⬜ **d** The student has used terms like 'might' or probably' in their answer, recognising that we cannot know for sure exactly why the interpretations are different.

⬜ **e** A good point about the answer is that the student has considered what 'side' the authors of the interpretations were on, and how this influenced their interpretations.

## DO IT!

Based on the following simplified version of the exam mark scheme, what level would you give this answer?

- Level 2 (3–4 marks): A developed answer that analyses provenance of interpretations to explain reasons for differences.

- Level 1 (1–2 marks): A simple answer that analyses provenance of interpretations to identify a reason or reasons for differences.

# Question 3

## About the question

Which interpretation do you find more convincing about...

Question 3 asks you which interpretation you find more convincing. It is worth 8 marks. Your task with this question is to use your own knowledge to evaluate each interpretation, decide which one you think is the most convincing and explain why.

## Answering the question

Here is one approach to answering Question 3.

**1** State the main argument of Interpretation A.

**2** Identify the most convincing part of that argument.

**3** Assess how convincing it is based on your own knowledge.

**4** State the main argument of Interpretation B.

**5** Identify the most convincing part of that argument.

**6** Assess how convincing it is based on your own knowledge.

**7** Make a judgement and back it up.

> **NAIL**IT!
>
> You don't have to completely agree with one interpretation and completely disagree with the other: your job is to decide which is more convincing.

**A** Overall, I find A more convincing about how successful Nazi economic policies were, because despite some of the ways in which the Nazis 'hid' unemployment, these did not cover up huge numbers of unemployed people, which means the Nazis were very successful in reducing unemployment between 1933 and 1939.

**B** This convinces me because I know that by 1939 there was almost full employment in Germany, with only 0.3 million unemployed compared to 6 million unemployed in 1933.

**C** However, B argues that the reduction in unemployment was not as significant as the Nazis claimed.

**D** The main argument of Interpretation A is that the combination of rearmament and the Nazis' job creation schemes were very successful in reducing unemployment in Germany.

**E** I find this quite convincing because I know that the Nazi government did change the way it counted unemployment in 1935 (part-time workers were counted as full-time), and forcing Jews out of government jobs and barring women from some jobs meant the state created unemployed people who then weren't counted as unemployed.

**F** The most convincing part of Interpretation A is when it provides details of the amount invested in rearmament and the millions of jobs this created.

**G** The most convincing part of Interpretation B is its claim that the Nazi state 'hid' a lot of unemployment.

> **DO**IT!
>
> Read the extracts from a student's answer to Question 3. What order should they go in to match the steps above?

Before you decide whether or not you find an interpretation convincing, you need to be clear about what it is saying – what its main argument is.

Read this interpretation, which is about the Reichstag elections of March 1933, two months after Hitler had become Chancellor of Germany.

---

**Interpretation A** Richard J. Evans, writing in his book *The Coming of the Third Reich*, written in 2004.

Richard Evans is a professor of history at Cambridge University who specialises in modern German history.

> Despite massive violence and intimidation, the Nazis had still managed to secure only 43.9 per cent of the vote [for the Reichstag elections of March 1933]. The Communists, unable to campaign, with their candidates in hiding or under arrest, still managed 12.3 per cent… Seventeen million people voted Nazi… but the electorate numbered almost 45 million. Nearly 5 million Communist votes, over 7 million Social Democrats, and a Centre Party vote of 5.5 million, testified to the complete failure of the Nazis, even under conditions of semi-dictatorship, to win over a majority of the electorate.

---

**Statements**

- **A** The Nazis had banned the Communists from taking part in the 1933 elections.
- **B** People did not feel forced to vote for the Nazi Party in 1933.
- **C** People still voted for parties that had actually been banned.
- **D** The Nazis secured (managed to get) a majority of votes in the 1933 elections.

**Arguments**

- **E** The Communists were still popular, even though they were banned and those standing for election had to hide from the police.
- **F** The Nazis failed to get a majority of votes, even when they controlled the elections.
- **G** Hitler would have to remove all political opposition to establish his dictatorship.
- **H** Nazi propaganda was not effective, otherwise more people would have voted for the Nazi Party in the 1933 elections.

**DO IT!**

1 Which of the statements A–D about Interpretation A are correct? Tick your choices.

2 Which one of the arguments E–H is the main argument of Interpretation A? Tick your answer.

**DO IT!**

It is a good idea to use a quote from each interpretation to evidence its main argument. What quote would you use from Interpretation A to evidence the author's main argument?

**NAIL IT!**

To access the higher levels (3 and 4) for Question 3, you need to analyse what you find convincing about both interpretations, rather than only really writing about one.

To work out how convincing you think each interpretation is, use your own knowledge about the question focus to check if you agree with its main argument or not.

If your own knowledge supports the interpretation, then it is more convincing. If what you know goes against the interpretation, then it is less convincing.

Read this interpretation, which is about the Gestapo: the Nazis' secret police force.

**Interpretation A** Jacques Delarue, writing in his book *The History of the Gestapo*, written in 1964.

Jacques Delarue was a member of the French Resistance during the Second World War. These were people who fought against the German occupation of France, and were hunted by the Gestapo.

> The Gestapo spotted or overheard every German's slightest movement. Never before, in no other land and at no other time, had an organisation achieved such a total penetration of society, possessed such power and been so able to arouse complete terror and horror, as well as in its actual effectiveness.

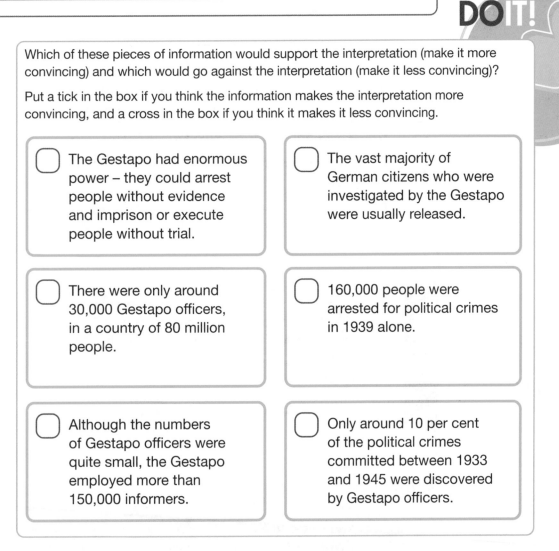

DO IT!

Which of these pieces of information would support the interpretation (make it more convincing) and which would go against the interpretation (make it less convincing)?

Put a tick in the box if you think the information makes the interpretation more convincing, and a cross in the box if you think it makes it less convincing.

◯ The Gestapo had enormous power – they could arrest people without evidence and imprison or execute people without trial.

◯ The vast majority of German citizens who were investigated by the Gestapo were usually released.

◯ There were only around 30,000 Gestapo officers, in a country of 80 million people.

◯ 160,000 people were arrested for political crimes in 1939 alone.

◯ Although the numbers of Gestapo officers were quite small, the Gestapo employed more than 150,000 informers.

◯ Only around 10 per cent of the political crimes committed between 1933 and 1945 were discovered by Gestapo officers.

Your answer to Question 3 should make a judgement about which interpretation you find more convincing.

You should also explain your judgement. Your explanation should link back to the information you used to evaluate the interpretations.

Here is another interpretation to go with the one about the Gestapo on the previous page.

> **Interpretation B** Laurence Rees, writing in his book *The Nazis: A Warning from History*, written in 2005.
>
> Laurence Rees is a historian who has also worked for the BBC on history programmes, including many on the Nazis.
>
> > Like all modern policing systems, the Gestapo was only as good or bad as the cooperation it received [from the public] – and the files reveal that it received a very high level of cooperation, making it a very good secret police force indeed… [A]round 80 per cent of all political crime was discovered by ordinary citizens who turned the information over to the police or the Gestapo. The files also show that most of this unpaid cooperation came from people who were not members of the Nazi Party – they were 'ordinary' citizens.

**DO IT!**

Which one of the student answers A–D best describes the main argument of Interpretation B? Tick your choice.

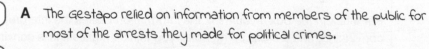

- [ ] **A** The Gestapo relied on information from members of the public for most of the arrests they made for political crimes.
- [ ] **B** The Gestapo was not a very effective secret police force.
- [ ] **C** The majority of German citizens were too frightened of the Gestapo to oppose Hitler or the Nazi regime.
- [ ] **D** There were actually very few Gestapo officers compared to the size of the German population.

**3** Which interpretation do you find more convincing about the role of the Gestapo in controlling the German people? Explain your answer using Interpretations A and B and your contextual knowledge

**(8 marks)**

**DO IT!**

Write an answer to this question using Interpretation A on the previous page and Interpretation B above. Make sure you include a judgement about which interpretation you find most convincing.

**NAIL IT!**

It is a good idea to repeat the words of the question when you are making your judgement, for example, 'Overall, I find A more convincing about the role of the Gestapo in controlling the German people because…'

# Question 4

## About the question

Describe two problems...

This question is worth 4 marks. You complete it by: using your knowledge to identify two problems with a specific issue, then developing your answer by describing in what ways it was a problem.

## Answering the question

Study the following issues for governments in Germany between 1890 and 1929. The problems alongside them are not in the right order.

1 Draw lines to connect relevant problems to each issue for government.

2 For each problem, describe why it was a problem for that issue. For example:

> Wealthy industrialists wanted to gain more political power from the Prussian elite, which was a problem for the government because it was led by Prussians, who wanted to hold on to their power.

**NAILIT!**

The difference between Level 1 and Level 2 for this question is that Level 1 shows knowledge (you identify two problems) while Level 2 shows knowledge and understanding (you extend your knowledge to show, for example, what made something problematic).

| Issues for government: | | Problems from the period 1890–1929: | |
|---|---|---|---|
| Dealing with the growth of parliamentary democracy | 1 | a | Germany could not drive the French and Belgians out because their army was too weak |
| Reacting to the impacts of the German Revolution, 1918–19 | 2 | b | International investors had lost confidence in the German mark |
| Tackling the occupation of the Ruhr | 3 | c | Germany's refusal to pay its reparations had damaged its international reputation |
| Combating political unrest 1919–23 | 4 | d | The abdication of the Kaiser meant a change from monarchy to republic |
| Bringing hyperinflation under control | 5 | e | Wealthy industrialists wanted to gain more political power from the Prussian elite |
| Repairing Germany's international situation | 6 | f | The new Weimar government was too weak on its own to put down the rebellions |

Look at the exam-style question below.

**4** Describe two problems faced by Hitler in establishing his dictatorship in 1933–34.

**(4 marks)**

## DO IT!

1 Select two problems to describe from this list. Caution: not everything in the list is relevant to this question.

   **a** The SA and Ernst Röhm      **d** Political opposition
   **b** Hitler becomes Führer        **e** The trade unions
   **c** Labour shortages           **f** Prussian militarism

2 Describe your **two** problems using this template:

> One problem for Hitler in establishing his dictatorship was...
> because...

Study this next exam-style question and the student answer that follows it.

**4** Describe two problems faced by Hitler in ruling Germany up to 1939.

**(4 marks)**

One of Hitler's biggest problems was rearming Germany ready to fight a war because Germany could not produce everything it needed and was having to spend money importing raw materials for rearmament such as oil. Hitler needed Germany to be self-sufficient in raw materials, otherwise its enemies could block Germany's ports and weaken it.

Another problem faced by Hitler was getting complete control over the Churches. The Churches had their own youth groups, which was a problem because Hitler wanted all young people to be in the Hitler Youth, under Nazi control and learning Nazi values.

## DO IT!

What level would you give this answer? Use the mark scheme below to help you.

### NAIL IT!
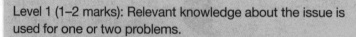

Level 1 (1–2 marks): Relevant knowledge about the issue is used for one or two problems.

Level 2 (3–4 marks): Both problems are described using relevant knowledge and both are supported by understanding that shows why they were problematic.

# Question 5

## About the question

 In what ways...

Question 5 is worth 8 marks. This question is about identifying changes and explaining the consequences of these changes for people or groups of people.

This question can be worded in a couple of different ways, for example:

- In what ways did the lives of people in Germany change during [X]?
- In what ways were the lives of people in Germany affected by [X]?

Instead of 'the lives of people in Germany' the question can also ask about a specific group of people, e.g. women in Germany, young people in Germany, German Jews, etc.

## Answering the question

Some possible changes for German people are listed in this diagram:

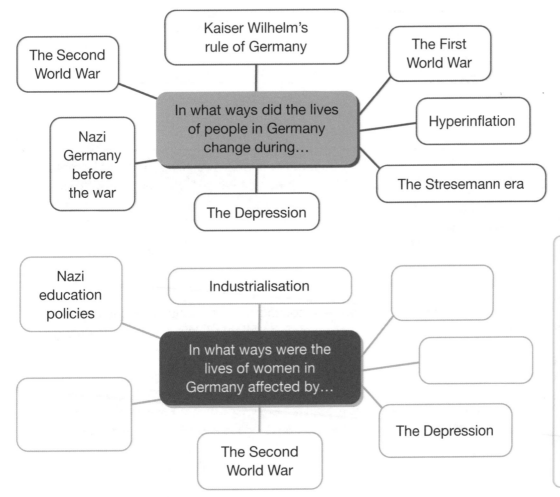

**NAIL**IT!

As you are revising Germany 1890–1945, try and think up your own Question 5s. For example, when you're revising the establishment of Hitler's dictatorship, you could ask: 'In what ways were the lives of workers in Germany affected by Hitler's policies on trade unions?'

**DO**IT!

Complete your own diagram for this question stem: 'In what ways were the lives of women in Germany affected by...' Try to add another three periods of change from the 1890–1945 course, using different periods from the ones in the diagram above, if you can.

## DO IT!

1 Identify a change that happened for people as a result of each of the following:

a The Nazi state's economic policies

b The Nazi state's social policies

c The Nazi state's racial policies and persecution.

2 The table on the right has a line under each change. Use this to fill in a consequence of each change – how were people's lives affected by the change?

A good way to approach Question 5 is to think of it as a question about change. Your first job is to identify changes. For example, as a result of the Depression, people who used to have jobs no longer had jobs.

Here are some examples of changes.

| | |
|---|---|
| **Industrialisation** | People who used to work on the land now worked in factories. |
| | |
| **The First World War** | By 1917, women made up nearly 30% of the workforce because of the millions of men who left work to fight in the war. |
| | |
| **Hyperinflation** | People who had saved up enough money to live on in their retirement now found that their savings were worth nothing at all. |
| | |
| **The Depression** | By early 1933, 6 million Germans had no job – over 25% of the working population had become unemployed. |
| | |
| **The Second World War** | Over 300,000 Germans were killed by Allied bombing and 3.6 million homes were destroyed: one-fifth of all Germany's housing. |
| | |

## NAIL IT!

Your answer for Question 5 should ideally identify and explain two or more consequences. You also need to support your explanations with relevant and accurate knowledge and understanding, which is what we'll look at next...

Your second step is to identify a consequence or consequences of the change for people. How were their lives affected as a result of the change? For example:

Social reforms under Kaiser Wilhelm's government meant working conditions improved in factories. This made life better for workers because, for example, after 1891 they no longer had to work on Sundays and could have a day off.

You need to support your explanation of consequences for people with relevant and accurate knowledge and understanding.

Here are examples of consequences (first table) and examples of supporting details (second table):

| | | |
|---|---|---|
| **A** As a consequence of Aryan ideas about a 'master race', people with mental and physical disabilities were discriminated against. | **B** As a result of Nazi anti-Semitism, German Jews were subjected to increasing discrimination and persecution. | **C** Young people's education changed, with boys and girls studying different subjects and being taught Nazi propaganda. |
| **D** Signing the Treaty of Versailles meant that Germans had to accept blame for starting the First World War. | **E** A consequence of Weimar culture was that women had more freedom to express themselves. | **F** One way in which the Enabling Act changed people's lives was that trade unions were made illegal. |

**DO**IT!

Match the consequences A–F (first table) with the correct supporting details U–Z (second table).

| | | |
|---|---|---|
| **U** The War Guilt Clause was Article 231 of the Treaty and was strongly resented by almost all Germans. | **V** Kristallnacht (9 November 1938) saw 91 Jews killed and 7000 Jewish businesses and 177 synagogues destroyed. | **W** For example, women went out on their own, drank and smoked in public, and wore more makeup. |
| **X** People with these conditions were sterilised (from 1933) so they could not have children. | **Y** The German Labour Front (DAF) was set up to manage workers' rights and wages, and all workers had to join. | **Z** For example, biology lessons included Nazi ideas about the superiority of the Aryan race. |

Sometimes consequences were different for different groups, or were different at different times. One example is that while women were encouraged to leave work by Nazi policies during peacetime, the Nazi state needed women to take on more work during the war because many men joined the armed forces.

**NAIL**IT!

Level 4 answers for Question 5 show a complex explanation of change, such as:

- how different changes happened at different times
- how there were different consequences for different groups
- how social impacts and economic impacts were different.

**DO**IT!

1 Explain how hyperinflation affected both people who were in a lot of debt and those who relied on their savings. Explain the different impact on these groups.

2 Explain why Nazi control over the Churches had different effects for Protestant Christians and for Catholic Christians in Germany.

Look at the exam-style question below.

> **5** In what ways were the lives of young people in Germany affected by Nazi social policies? Explain your answer.
>
> **(8 marks)**

Now read this example answer to the question.

**a** A good point is that the student wrote about more than one change – the Hitler Youth plus this second change.

**b** The student supports their answer with evidence to show their knowledge and understanding. For example, they give evidence about what was different from youth organisations in the past.

**c** The student has referred to relevant Nazi social policies on school education and this other policy.

**d** The student makes a good attempt here to explain how young people's lives were changed by this policy.

**e** This explanation is quite simple and does not explain how the change affected young people's lives.

The Nazi Party changed young people's lives by making them join the Hitler Youth, which was how they convinced young people that Hitler was great and everyone should do what he said and hate Jews. This was different for young people because before they might have been in different youth organisations, e.g. Catholic ones that were about being good and kind to other people.

Another change was that girls did some different subjects at school than boys, for example girls did cooking and needlework, which was to train them to be housewives.

## DO IT!

1 Draw lines to connect the statements labelled a–e to the parts of the student's answer they apply to.

2 Based on the simplified version of the exam mark scheme below, what level would you give this answer?

## NAIL IT!

Level 1: Basic – the student identifies a change that is relevant to the question.

Level 2: Simple – the student identifies a change or changes and backs one up with relevant knowledge.

Level 3: Developed – the student identifies and develops explanations of two or more changes, supporting both with relevant and accurate knowledge.

Level 4: Complex – the student adds an explanation of complexities of change to a Level 3 answer.

# Question 6

## About the question

Which of the following was the more important reason why something happened?

This question asks which was the more important reason why something happened? It is worth 12 marks, roughly a quarter of the paper. You need to explain how both reasons in Question 6 *caused something*: this is called explanation of causation.

## Answering the question

Some key causes are: political reasons, economic reasons, social reasons and cultural reasons.

Below are some causes (reasons why things happened) in Germany, 1890–1945 (top table) and some developments (things that happened) in Germany, 1890–1945 (bottom table).

**Causes**

| Poverty in the Depression | The growth in socialism | Introduction of a new currency |
|---|---|---|
| Papen's deal to get Nazi support in the Reichstag | The hyperinflation crisis | Aryan ideas |

**Developments**

| Hitler's decision to launch the Munich Putsch in 1923 | Growth in support for the Nazi Party 1928–32 | Difficulties in ruling Germany 1890–1914 |
|---|---|---|
| Recovery during the Stresemann era, 1924–29 | Increasing persecution of Jewish Germans 1933–39 | Hitler becoming Chancellor in 1933 |

### NAILIT!

When you are revising for this paper, think about causes in terms of economic, political, social or cultural. This will help you tackle explanation of causation questions.

### DOIT!

1 Match the causes (top table) to the developments (bottom table).

2 Sort the reasons (top table) into political, economic, social and cultural. Some may belong to more than one category, e.g. economic and social.

Question 6 will always list two reasons for you to analyse. These are often quite 'broad' causes such as 'economic policies' or 'social changes' or 'religion'. Sometimes one or both may be a bit more specific, such as 'Prussian militarism' or 'Hitler's appeal'. That means there will usually be different factors to unpack and use in your answer.

Here are six reasons for the recovery during the Stresemann era (1924–29):

| | | |
|---|---|---|
| Strict controls on how many Rentenmarks the government could print | Reparation payments were reduced to what Germany should be able to pay | Back up for the Rentenmark – if it failed, investors would get compensation in land |
| Germany agreed to respect the borders between itself, Belgium and France | The USA loaned Germany $200 million | The total amount of reparations was reduced to £1850 million. |

### NAILIT!

When you are able to unpack a 'broad' reason to show there were several different factors involved, you are showing your knowledge and understanding of the period. There are 6 marks available in this question for showing your knowledge and understanding in this way. (The other 6 marks are for your explanation, analysis and judgement skills.)

## DOIT!

1 Foreign policy was important in explaining why there was a recovery during the Stresemann era. Which of the reasons in this table are foreign policy reasons?

2 For each of the foreign policy reasons you have identified, explain why they were important for the recovery during the Stresemann era (1924–29).

### NAILIT!

It is important in this question to 'explain why X was important for Y'. For example, 'why foreign policy was important for the recovery during the Stresemann era'. You need to *stretch* your explanation to do this. For example, if you say, 'Reducing reparations was important because it made reparations easier for Germany to afford', then you have not *stretched* your explanation to cover *why this was important for the recovery during the Stresemann era.*

Your explanations of causation in Question 6 need to be supported with relevant factual knowledge (e.g. facts and figures) and understanding (e.g. details, developments).

Here are four points about importance followed by six pieces of evidence from across your Germany 1890–1945 option.

## Points about importance

**1** The growth of socialism was such an important threat that the Kaiser's government brought in social reforms to improve conditions for workers.

**2** The most important reason for the German revolution was the shortage of food.

**3** One of the most resented aspects of the Treaty of Versailles was the loss of territory.

**4** The Depression had such an important impact on German society because almost all families became poorer.

## Pieces of evidence

- There were 1.8 million unemployed at the start of 1929. By 1933, over 6 million Germans were unemployed.

- There were benefits for workers who could not work because of illness (1903) and laws to prevent children under 13 from working in factories (1908).

- 750,000 Germans died in 1918 because they could not get enough to eat.

- These lands had produced 50 per cent of all Germany's iron ore, 15 per cent of its coal and 15 per cent of its farm production.

- By 1914, around 2.5 million Germans belonged to trade unions.

- At one point in 1923, it cost 4 billion German marks to buy a dozen eggs.

**DO**IT!

**1** Match a piece of evidence to each of the four points about importance.

**2** Find evidence from the revision section of this book, or your own knowledge, to back up these four statements about importance:

- In my opinion, the most important reason for the failure of Weimar democracy was the massive increase in votes for extremist parties that rejected democracy.

- In my opinion, the main reason for the Reichstag passing the Enabling Act was Hitler's ban on the KPD after the Reichstag Fire.

- The continuing support for the Nazi regime was not just because of repression and control: Hitler had promised to abolish unemployment, and he achieved this.

- I consider fear of repression to be more important than propaganda in explaining why there was not very much opposition to the Nazi regime before the war.

Question 6 asks you to make a judgement: which of the two reasons was more important. Either of the two can be the most important – there isn't one 'right' answer. What you need to do is explain why you consider one reason to be more important than the other.

Here are some possible arguments to consider in deciding why one reason may be more important than the other reason:

- One reason affected more people than the other.

- One reason caused the other reason.

- One reason caused more consequences than the other.

**DO IT!**

Read these three judgements. Which argument is each using to make its judgement?

**1**

In my opinion, radio was the most important reason why propaganda was so effective in Nazi Germany, because radio broadcasts reached so many people. The Nazis boosted production of cheap radio sets so that by 1939, 70 per cent of German families owned a radio - the highest percentage of radio ownership in any country in the world.

**2**

Fear of communism was more important than economic problems in explaining why support for the Nazi Party grew. The Catholic Church and Centre Party gave their support to the Nazis because of fear of communism. Middle-class people were terrified that communists would take away their nice way of life. Farmers were worried that communists would take their farms and set low food prices. Big business was worried that communists would nationalise their industries. German people had faced severe poverty before without this turning into support for the Nazis, for example in 1923.

**3**

It is clear that industrialisation was more important than the growth of parliamentary government in explaining why Kaiser Wilhelm struggled to rule Germany. Parliamentary government was only a problem because industrialisation had: weakened the power of the Prussian elite; increased the wealth and influence of German industrialists, who now wanted a share in governing Germany; and created a working class, with voting rights, who wanted to use the Reichstag to improve their working conditions and pay.

**NAIL IT!**

The most successful answers for Question 6 consider how the two reasons given in the question connected with each other or influenced each other. This makes the answer more complex, which is why the top level of the mark scheme for Question 6 is called 'complex explanation'.

Look at the exam-style question below.

**6** Which of the following was the more important reason why there was only limited opposition to Hitler in the years 1933–1939:

- Propaganda
- The Gestapo?

Explain your answer with reference to **both** reasons.

**(12 marks)**

Now read this example answer to the question. There are several ways in which this answer could be improved: can you spot them?

The Gestapo was important because it made people frightened of the Nazi state so that they followed the rules. The Gestapo was a secret police force which meant they could spy on people and put them in prison and even torture them or execute them without any trial. The Gestapo was part of the SS and the head of the SS and the other police forces was Heinrich Himmler. Propaganda was important as well, because it helped Hitler win elections, such as in 1930 and 1932.

**Common weaknesses checklist**

☐ Only explaining the importance of one reason

☐ Not relating importance to the question focus (i.e. to why there was only limited opposition to Hitler)

☐ Not supporting the explanations with evidence

☐ Not using relevant evidence to support the explanations

☐ Not making a judgement

**NAIL**IT!

An answer like this one would probably get a Level 1 mark. Level 1 (1–3 marks) recognises that the answer gives a basic explanation of one or both bullets, using basic knowledge and understanding.

**DO**IT!

1 Read the checklist of common weaknesses that stop students from doing as well as they should on Question 6. Tick which ones you think apply to the answer above.

2 Write feedback on this answer that includes at least *three* pointers as to how it could be improved. For example, 'Your answer should have explained the importance of both reasons. A point you could have considered for propaganda was that Germans were constantly being told that Hitler was all that was stopping Germany from a communist takeover.'

3 Now try and write your own complete answer to the exam-style question above. Look back over pages 63–66, as well as this page, to remind yourself of what answers to Question 6 need to do.

Compare your answer to the question on the previous page with the following student answer to the same question.

On the one hand, propaganda was an important reason why there was only limited opposition to Hitler. One of the types of opposition to Hitler was the Edelweiss Pirates, but there were only ever around 2000 Pirates compared to 8 million members of the Hitler Youth in 1939. Hitler wanted all young people in Germany to be surrounded by Nazi propaganda all the way through their youth, so that they would be completely indoctrinated with Nazi ideas and would worship Hitler without question. That is why everyone in the Hitler Youth swore an oath of loyalty to Hitler. And it wasn't only young people who were surrounded by propaganda: 60 per cent of all German newspapers were owned by the Nazis by 1939, which meant they were full of propaganda about how well Hitler was doing and what a great leader he was. The Nazi state had also boosted production of cheap radios and encouraged German families to buy a radio set, so by 1939 70 per cent of families had one. But the radios could only pick up German stations and these were controlled by the Nazis, so again the only news most Germans ever heard before the war was propaganda. Therefore propaganda was important because it made it very difficult for people to think that Hitler could be wrong about anything, let alone get involved in opposition to Hitler.

On the other hand, the Gestapo was also a reason why Germans did not oppose Hitler. Germans were very frightened of the Gestapo because they could arrest people based just on suspicion, and then they could torture people to make them confess, and then send them to concentration camps or even execute them without there being any trial or opportunity for their victims to prove they were innocent. This fear of the Gestapo would have stopped people from opposing Hitler because of the danger of being arrested. However, there were only ever around 30,000 Gestapo officers in Germany, which had 80 million people, which meant the Gestapo relied on ordinary people informing on others about political offences - such as disrespecting Hitler by telling a joke about him. There could be many different reasons why a person would inform on someone, but in my view a lot of Germans informed on others because they believed Nazi propaganda and wanted Hitler to stay in charge.

To conclude, propaganda was more important than the Gestapo in explaining why there was only limited opposition to Hitler. The Gestapo was an important factor because people were terrified of being arrested by the Gestapo, and this would have stopped people from opposing Hitler. But propaganda was more important because it meant most Germans believed in Hitler and wanted him to continue his policies. Propaganda explains why the Gestapo was effective, because, with limited numbers of officers, the Gestapo relied on ordinary Germans informing on their neighbours if they did not show enough respect to Hitler.

> Note how the student has **related their explanation to the question focus**. Note also how they have used **relevant supporting details** to show their knowledge and understanding.

**DO IT!**

Which of the levels from the mark scheme would you give this answer?

**Level 1**: Basic explanation one or both of the bullets (reasons).

**Level 2**: Simple explanation of the bullets using specific knowledge and understanding.

**Level 3**: Developed explanation of both bullets that uses a range of accurate and relevant knowledge and understanding.

**Level 4**: Complex explanation of both bullets that uses that uses a range of accurate and relevant knowledge and understanding, and makes a judgement about which was the more important reason.

# Practice Papers

## Practice Paper 1

**01** Read **Interpretations A** and **B**.

How does **Interpretation B** differ from **Interpretation A** about what young Germans thought of the Hitler Youth?

Explain your answer using **Interpretations A** and **B**.

**(4 marks)**

**02** Why might the authors of **Interpretations A** and **B** have a different interpretation about what young Germans thought of the Hitler Youth?

Explain your answer using **Interpretations A** and **B** and your contextual knowledge.

**(4 marks)**

**03** Which interpretation do you find more convincing about what young Germans thought of the Hitler Youth?

Explain your answer using **Interpretations A** and **B** and your contextual knowledge.

**(8 marks)**

**04** Describe two problems faced by Weimar governments in ruling Germany between 1919 and 1923.

**(4 marks)**

**05** In what ways did the lives of people in Germany change during the Depression (1929–1933)?

Explain your answer.

**(8 marks)**

**06** Which of the following was the more important reason why Germany was difficult to govern in the years 1890–1914:

- the upper class
- the working class?

Explain your answer with reference to **both** reasons.

**(12 marks)**

### Interpretations for use with Practice paper 1

Interpretation A Melita Maschmann, writing in her book *Account Rendered*, written in 1963.

Maschmann secretly joined the Hitler Youth in 1933, when she was 15, against her parents' wishes. After the war she wrote a memoir of her time as a Nazi supporter. The memoir is written in the form of a letter to a Jewish classmate of hers who she felt guilty about.

> [A]s my parents would not allow me to become a member of the Hitler Youth I joined secretly… But what now awaited me was a bitter disappointment, the extent of which I dared not admit to myself. The evening meetings for which we met in a dark and grimy cellar were fatally lacking in interest. The time was passed in paying subscriptions, drawing up countless lists and swotting up the words of songs… Discussions on political texts from, say, *Mein Kampf*, quickly ended in general silence.

Interpretation B Erich Dressler, writing in his book *Nine Lives Under the Nazis*, in 2011.

Erich Dressler was born in 1924. His mother had suffered from poverty under the Weimar Republic and Erich became an enthusiastic Nazi supporter, helping to get rid of unpopular teachers at his school and taking part in Kristallnacht in 1938.

> Father used to say the most shocking things about the Führer. So I did not tell him about the Jungvolk [Hitler Youth], but I joined it all the same – and with it began for me the greatest experience of my life… We had group meetings with community singing, story-telling and reading. And whatever was read to us was well-chosen. It was invariably picked from German history, and it is only proper, most of it was about the many great soldiers which our nation has produced.

# Practice Paper 2

**01** Read **Interpretations A** and **B**.

How does **Interpretation B** differ from **Interpretation A** about the reasons why Germans supported Hitler?

Explain your answer using **Interpretations A** and **B**.

**(4 marks)**

**02** Why might the authors of **Interpretations A** and **B** have a different interpretation about the reasons why Germans supported Hitler?

Explain your answer using **Interpretations A** and **B** and your contextual knowledge.

**(4 marks)**

**03** Which interpretation do you find more convincing about the reasons why Germans supported Hitler?

Explain your answer using **Interpretations A** and **B** and your contextual knowledge.

**(8 marks)**

**04** Describe two problems faced by Hitler in establishing a dictatorship in Germany in the years 1933 to 1934.

**(4 marks)**

**05** In what ways did the lives of people in Germany change during the Stresemann era (1924–1929)?

Explain your answer.

**(8 marks)**

**06** Which of the following was the more important reason for growth in support for the Nazis between 1928 and 1932:

- the Depression
- Hitler's appeal?

Explain your answer with reference to **both** reasons.

**(12 marks)**

### Interpretations for use with Practice paper 2

Interpretation A Christopher Isherwood, writing in his book *Goodbye to Berlin*, written in 1939.

Christopher Isherwood was 25 years old when he went to live in Berlin in 1929. He worked there as an English teacher, enjoying the vibrant nightlife and observing the end of the Weimar Republic. His stories about Berlin cover a period from 1930 to 1933.

> This morning I even heard [his landlady] Mrs Schroeder talking reverently about 'The Führer' to the porter's wife. If anyone were to remind her that, at the elections last November, she voted communist, she would probably deny it hotly, and in perfect good faith. She is merely acclimatizing herself, in accordance with a natural law, like an animal which changes its coat in winter. Thousands of people like Mrs Schroeder are acclimatising themselves. After all, whatever government is in power, they are doomed to live in this town.

Interpretation B W.E.B. DuBois, writing in an American newspaper article 'What of the Color-Line?' in 1940.

W.E.B. DuBois was an African American academic who visited Germany for six months in the 1930s. He described his experiences in an American weekly newspaper, the *Pittsburgh Courier*, which was aimed at African American readers.

> Hitler made the vast majority of Germans believe that his way was the only way and that it was actually leading to the promised land. Nine out of every ten Germans believe this today, and as long as they are convinced of this, they are going to uphold Hitler at any cost. They know the cost which they pay and they hate it. They hate war, they hate spying, they hate the loss of their liberties. But in return for this immense sacrifice, they have… a nation at work, after a nightmare of unemployment.

# Doing well in your exam

This revision guide is designed to help you with Section A of your **Paper 1: Understanding the Modern World** exam.

**Section A** is the **Period Study** which will be accompanied by an **Interpretations Booklet**.

**Section B** is the **Wider World Study** which will be accompanied by a **Sources Booklet**.

You will have an answer booklet for Sections A and B, an interpretations booklet for Section A and a sources booklet for Section B. Check that you have the correct booklets for the topics you studied.

## Assessment objectives

Your answers will be marked according to a mark scheme based on four assessment objectives (AOs). AOs are set by Ofqual and are the same across all GCSE History specifications and all exam boards:

| AO1 | demonstrate knowledge and understanding of the key features and characteristics of the period studied. |
|---|---|
| AO2 | explain and analyse historical events and periods studied using second-order historical concepts (cause and consequence). |
| AO3 | analyse, evaluate and use sources (contemporary to the period) to make substantiated judgements, in the context of historical events studied. |
| AO4 | analyse, evaluate and make substantiated judgements about interpretations (including how and why interpretations may differ) in the context of historical events studied. |

Paper 1 Section A, covered in this guide, examines AO1, AO2, and AO4. There are no marks awarded for SPaG (Spelling, Punctuation and Grammar) in Paper 1 Section A.

You must <u>revise all of the content</u> from the specification as the questions in your exam could be on *any* of the topics listed. This guide is modelled on the specification so make sure you cover **all** the topics in this book.

There are six different types of question to answer in Section A:

| | |
|---|---|
| Question 1 | You will be given **two** interpretations: Interpretation A and Interpretation B. Question 1 will ask you about how the interpretations differ (how they are different). The wording of the question will be, 'How does Interpretation B differ from Interpretation A about…' Explain your answer using Interpretations A and B. |
| Best answers… | will identify a difference (or differences) between the two interpretations and then explain that difference based on the content of the interpretations. |
| (4 marks) *10 minutes* | The answer carries 4 marks so you do not have to write much. All 4 marks are for AO4. You will have approximately 10 minutes to answer this question. |

| | |
|---|---|
| **Question 2** | This question builds on Question 1: it asks you to suggest reasons why Interpretation A and Interpretation B are different. The wording of the question will be, 'Why might the authors of Interpretation A and B have a different interpretation about…' Explain your answer using the Interpretations A and B and your contextual knowledge. |
| Best answers… | will identify and explain reasons for the difference in the interpretations by analysing the provenance of the interpretations. You could try using the following method to help you remember what to include for provenance: |
| | <table><tr><td>**Who**</td><td>Who wrote it?</td></tr><tr><td>**When**</td><td>When did they write it?</td></tr><tr><td>**Where**</td><td>Where was it written?</td></tr><tr><td>**Why**</td><td>Why was it written?</td></tr><tr><td>**What**</td><td>What is it?</td></tr></table> |
| | It isn't possible to know for sure why interpretations are different, which is why it is a good idea to use phrases like 'this suggests that…' or 'this might be because…' |
| (4 marks) 5 minutes | There are 4 marks for this question. Like Question 1, all 4 marks are for AO4. You should spend no more than about 5 minutes on this question. |
| **Question 3** | This question builds on Questions 1 and 2. It is about how convincing you find both interpretations. The wording of the question will be, 'Which interpretation do you find more convincing about …? Explain your answer using the Interpretations A and B and your contextual knowledge. |
| Best answers… | will use your own knowledge to evaluate each interpretation, decide which one you think is the most convincing, and explain why. A good approach is first to state what the main argument of Interpretation A is, identify using your own contextual knowledge what you find convincing about it and what your own knowledge tells you is not so convincing (maybe it doesn't cover something relevant that you know about), then do the same for Interpretation B. Finally, use this analysis to make a judgement about which interpretation you find most convincing. |
| (8 marks) 10 minutes | The answer carries 8 marks. All 8 marks are for AO4. You will have approximately 10 minutes to answer this question. |
| **Question 4** | This question is not connected to Questions 1, 2 or 3. It will ask you to describe **two** problems about something from the course: it is worded like this, 'Describe two problems…' |
| Best answers… | will identify two different problems and then describe in what ways each one was a problem. |
| (4 marks) 5 minutes | There are 4 marks for this question so you do not need to write much. The 4 marks are all for AO1. You should spend no more than about 5 minutes on this question. |

| | |
|---|---|
| **Question 5** | This question is about identifying changes and explaining the consequences of these changes for people or groups of people. This question can be worded in a couple of different ways, for example:<br><br>• In what ways did the lives of people in Germany change during [X]?<br>• In what ways were the lives of people in Germany affected by [X]? |
| Best answers… | will identify changes and consequences. A good way to approach Question 5 is to think of it as a question about change. Therefore, the first job is to identify changes. Then identify a consequence or consequences of the change for the group of people in the question. How were their lives affected as a result of the change? You need to support your explanation of consequences for people with relevant and accurate knowledge and understanding. |
| **(8 marks)**<br>*10 minutes* | This question is worth 8 marks. 4 of the marks are for AO1 and 4 marks are for AO2. You will have approximately 10 minutes to answer this question. |
| **Question 6** | This question asks which of **two** reasons was the more important reason why something happened. The question will ask you to explain your answer with reference to *both* reasons. |
| Best answers… | to this essay question will explain how both reasons in Question 6 caused something: this is called explanation of causation. Some key causes are: political reasons, economic reasons, social reasons and cultural reasons. Explanations of causation need to be supported with relevant factual knowledge (e.g. facts and figures) and understanding (e.g. details, developments). Finally, make a judgement: which of the two reasons was more important? Either of the two can be the most important – there isn't one 'right' answer. What you need to do is explain why you consider one reason to be more important than the other. |
| **(12 marks)**<br>*15 minutes* | There are 12 marks for this question: 6 marks for AO1 and 6 marks for AO2. This question carries the most marks and therefore you should make sure you leave enough time to write your best answer. You will need to spend around 15 minutes on this question. |

Find past papers and mark schemes, and specimen papers on the AQA
website at www.aqa.org.uk/pastpapers

# Glossary

**abdicate** To step down from a position of leadership.

**armistice** An agreement to stop fighting (it does not necessarily end a war and it doesn't set peace terms).

**Aryan race** A term used from the 19th century for a mythical race of white people whose descendants were believed to be superior to all other races.

**autobahn** German name for dual-carriage motorways.

**censorship** Controlling the content of the media such as books, newspapers and films.

**communist** A left-wing **socialist** revolutionary.

**concentration camp** A prison camp where large numbers are held in a relatively small space and poor conditions.

**conscription** when the state makes it compulsory for people to join the armed forces.

**constitution** The laws or rules that state how a country is governed.

**depression** A serious and prolonged period of **economic** decline.

**emigrate** To leave your own country and settle permanently in another.

**ersatz** A product made or used as an inferior substitute for something else.

**Freikorps** Groups of ex-soldiers who refused to hand back their weapons after the First World War ended.

**Führer** A German word for leader, Hitler took this title when he combined the roles of Chancellor and President of Germany.

**Gestapo** Nazi plain clothes secret state police force.

**ghetto** A part of a city, often with poor quality housing, populated by a minority group.

**industrialisation** when a country's economy becomes dominated by industries rather than farming.

**Kaiser** German 'emperor' or royal leader.

**nationalism** when people identify with their nation more than anything else, e.g. 'I'm a German first and a working-class person second'

**Nazis** Members of Hitler's right-wing political party, the National Socialist German Worker's Party.

**persecution** Hostility, usually directed at someone due to their race or beliefs.

**propaganda** Spreading biased information and ideas to promote a cause.

**Prussian** someone from the German state of Prussia (Berlin was Prussia's capital).

**putsch** A violent attempt to overthrow the rightful government.

**rationing** When the government limits the amount that people can buy of products that are in short supply, for example, sugar, petrol, soap, to make sure supplies don't run out.

**raw materials** A basic material from which a product is made.

**refugee** someone forced to leave their home or country, often because of war.

**Reichstag** German parliament.

**reparations** Compensation paid by the losers of a war to the victors.

**repression** severe and cruel control of how people behave.

**sabotage** To damage an enemy's equipment, supplies, communications, etc. in secret so they cannot be used.

**self-sufficient** The ability to support or provide for oneself.

**socialist** One who believes the role of the state is to benefit the working man.

**social reforms** changes to laws that bring in better living and working conditions.

**SPD** Social Democratic Party, the largest party in the **Reichstag** in 1918.

**Star of David** A six pointed figure used as a Jewish symbol.

**tariff** A tax or payment made to import or export something.

**trade union** Organised body of workers.

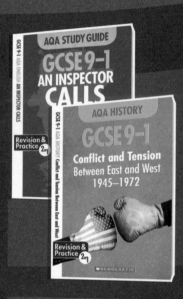